LLE

2007

Witches'
Spell-A-Day
Almanac

Holidays & Lore   Spells & Recipes
Rituals & Meditations

Copyright 2006 Llewellyn Worldwide.
Editing: K. M. Brielmaier; Design: Michael Fallon
Cover Design: Lisa Novak; Background Photo: © PhotoDisc
Interior Art: © 2005, Terry Miura (illustrations: pp. 9, 29, 47, 69, 89, 111, 131,
151, 171, 191, 211, 231); © 2005 Eris Klein (holiday and day icons)

You can order Llewellyn books and annuals from *New Worlds*, Llewellyn's
magazine catalog. To request a free copy of the catalog, call toll-free
1-877-NEW WRLD, or visit our website at http://subscriptions.llewellyn.com.

ISBN 0-7387-0333-8
Llewellyn is a registered trademark of Llewellyn Worldwide, Ltd.
2143 Wooddale Drive, Dept. 0-7387-0333-8
Woodbury, MN 55125

Table of Contents

About the Authors

Elizabeth Barrette serves as the managing editor of *PanGaia*. She has been involved with the Pagan community for more than seventeen years, and has done much networking with Pagans in her area. Her other writing fields include speculative fiction and gender studies. She lives in central Illinois and enjoys herbal landscaping and gardening for wildlife.

Boudica is reviews editor and co-owner of the *Wiccan/Pagan Times* and owner of the *Zodiac Bistro*, two online publications. She is a teacher with CroneSpeak, teaching both on and off the Internet, and guest speaker at many festivals and gatherings. A former New Yorker, she now resides with her husband in Ohio.

Ellen Dugan, the "Garden Witch," is the author of several Llewellyn books, including *Garden Witchery*, *Elements of Witchcraft*, *Cottage Witchery*, *Autumn Equinox*, *The Enchanted Cat*, *Herb Magic for Beginners*, and the forthcoming *Natural Witchery*.

Ember is a freelance writer and poet who follows the path of earth-centered spirituality. Her work has been published in *newWitch* and *PanGaia* magazines and in several Llewellyn annuals. She lives in the midwest with her husband of ten years.

Emely Flak is a solitary Witch from Daylesford, Australia. When she is not writing, she is a learning and development professional. Recently, this mother of two and partner of one completed training to be a civil celebrant. Much of her work is dedicated to embracing the ancient wisdom of Wicca for personal empowerment, particularly in the competitive work environment.

Lily Gardner continues to pursue and write about her lifelong passion for folklore and mythology. She has been a practicing Witch for thirteen years. In addition to her work in folklore, she writes short stories and is working on her first mystery novel. Lily lives with her husband in the rainy but magnificent city of Portland, Oregon.

James Kambos is a writer and folk artist. He holds a degree in history and has had a lifelong interest in folk magic. He has authored numerous articles on the folk magic traditions of Greece, the Near East, and the Appalachian region of the United States. He makes his home in the beautiful hill country of southern Ohio.

Kristin Madden is a best-selling author of several books on parenting, shamanism, and Paganism, including the Llewellyn titles *The Book of Shamanic Healing*

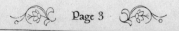

and *Dancing the Goddess Incarnate*. A Druid and tutor in the Order of Bards, Ovates, and Druids, she is also dean of the Ardantane School of Shamanic Studies. Kristin and her work have appeared in print and on radio and television throughout North America and Europe.

Sharynne NicMhacha is a Canadian writer, teacher, and bard of Scottish and Irish ancestry. She has studied Celtic languages and mythology through Harvard University, and has presented work at the University of Edinburgh, University College Cork, and the Omega Institute.

Olivia O'Meir is a feminist Dianic Witch, priestess of the Goddess, and ordained reverend from the Philadelphia area. She is a craftswoman, free-lance writer, tarot counselor, and sister in the Coven of the Five Sisters. Her studies focus on the Goddess, geology, mythology, and Avalon.

Paniteowl lives in the foothills of the Appalachians in northeast Pennsylvania, where she and her husband are in the process of developing a private retreat for spiritual awareness. She is co-coordinator of two annual events in Virginia known as the Gathering of the Tribes. She is founder and elder high priestess of the Mystic Wicca tradition.

Laurel Reufner has been a solitary Pagan for over a decade. She is active in the local CUUPS chapter, Circle of Gaia Dreaming, and is often attracted to bright and shiny ideas. Southeastern Ohio has always been home, where she currently lives in lovely Athens County with her wonderful husband and two adorable heathens, er, daughters.

Cerridwen Iris Shea is a writer, teacher, and tarot reader who loves ice hockey and horse racing. She is a longtime contributor to Llewellyn's almanacs and calendars.

Tammy Sullivan is a full-time writer and solitary Witch who writes from her home in the foothills of the Great Smokey Mountains. She is the author of *Pagan Anger Magic; Positive Transformations from Negative Energies*, and *Elemental Witch*.

Gail Wood has been a Witch and Wiccan priestess for more than twenty years, practicing a shamanic path celebrating the Dark Moon. She is clergy, teacher, ritual leader, tarot reader, and Reiki Master. She is the author of *Rituals of the Dark Moon: 13 Lunar Rites for a Magical Path* and *The Wild God: Meditations and Rituals on the Sacred Masculine*.

Introduction

A Note on Magic and Spells

The spells in the *Witches' Spell-A-Day Almanac* evoke everyday magic designed to improve our lives and homes. You needn't be an expert on magic to follow these simple rites and spells; as you will see if you use these spells through the year, magic, once mastered, is easy to perform. The only advanced technique required of you is the art of visualization.

Visualization is an act of controlled imagination. If you can call up in your mind a picture of your best friend's face or a flag flapping in the breeze, you can visualize. In magic, visualizations are used to direct and control magical energies. Basically, the spell-caster creates a visual image of the spell's desired goal, whether it be perfect health, a safe house, or a protected pet.

Visualization is the basis of all good spells, and as such it is a tool that should be properly used. Visualization must be real in the mind of the spell-caster so that it allows him or her to raise, concentrate, and send forth energy to accomplish the spell.

Perhaps when visualizing you'll find that you're doing everything right, but you don't feel anything. This is common, for we haven't been trained to acknowledge—let alone utilize—our magical abilities. Keep practicing, however, for your spells can "take" even if you're not the most experienced natural magician.

You will notice also that many spells in this collection have a somewhat "light" tone. They are seemingly fun and frivolous, filled with rhyme and colloquial speech. This is not to diminish the seriousness of the purpose, but rather to create a relaxed atmosphere for the practitioner. Lightness of spirit helps focus energy; rhyme and common language help the spell-caster remember the words and train the mind where it is needed. The intent of this magic is indeed very serious at times; and magic is never to be trifled with.

Even when your spells are effective, magic won't usually sparkle before your very eyes. The test of magic's success is time, not immediate eye-popping results. But you can feel magic's energy for yourself by rubbing your palms together briskly for ten seconds, then holding them a few

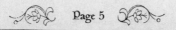

inches apart. Sense the energy passing through them, the warm tingle in your palms. This is the power raised and used in magic. It comes from within and is perfectly natural.

Among the features of the *Witches' Spell-A-Day Almanac* are an easy-to-use "book of days" format; new spells specifically tailored for each day of the year (and its particular magical, astrological, and historical energies); and additional tips and lore for various days throughout the year—including color correspondences based on planetary influences, obscure and forgotten holidays and festivals, and an incense-of-the-day to help you waft magical energies from the ether into your space.

In creating this product, we were inspired by the ancient almanac traditions and the layout of the classic nineteenth-century almanac *Chamber's Book of Days*, which is subtitled *A Miscellany of Popular Antiquities in connection with the Calendar*. As you will see, our fifteen authors this year made history a theme of their spells, and we hope that by knowing something of the magic of past years we may make our current year all the better.

Enjoy your days, and have a magical year!

2007
Year of Spells

January is the first month of the Gregorian calendar. Its name comes from the two-faced Roman god Janus, ruler of gates and doorways. Its astrological sign Capricorn, the goat (December 21–January 20), is a cardinal earth sign ruled by Saturn. January is a time of new beginnings. New Year's Day brings with it the tradition of making resolutions for the year. Popular customs include opening the front and back doors of the home, a symbolic way of letting the new year in and the old year out. Epiphany, or Twelfth Night, falls on January 6 and is the final night of the Christmas season. This night is a time to gather family and friends near a crackling fire, enjoying food and sweets and sharing hopes and wishes for the coming year. January's Full Moon was known as the Wolf Moon, a time when the hungry pack would search for food. In many regions, snow blankets the ground, icicles hang from the eaves, and the night sky is spangled with starlight. Evergreen trees, symbols of eternal life, stand out now in the winter woodland. Bluejays and cardinals brighten the winter landscape. Traditionally during this month Pagans perform purification magic using seasonal scents such as pine and ginger. The ritual burning of written charms so that their magic may be released is also popular in January.

January 1
Monday

New Year's Day – Kwanzaa ends

 2nd ♊
Color of the day: Gray
Incense of the day: Poplar

Fresh Beginning Spell

Today marks a fresh beginning. Use this time to reflect on your accomplishments from the last year, and set goals for the year to come. What were your New Year's resolutions last January? How many of them did you keep? If you're like most of us, you managed to keep some but not all. Here is a spell to improve your chances this year. You'll need a piece of parchment paper and a pen—preferably a quill pen with a bottle of ink to dip it in. Write out your New Year's resolutions; four is a good number. Sign your magical name underneath. Then say:

> Out with the old
> And in with the new!
> Remind me what
> I have sworn to do,
> And give me the
> Strength to follow
> through.

Roll up the list and tie with a brown ribbon, for grounding. Keep it on your altar until next year.

Elizabeth Barrette

Holiday lore: New Year's Day calls for safeguards, augurs, charms, and proclamations. All over the world on this day, people kiss strangers, shoot guns into the air, toll bells, and exchange gifts. Preferred gifts are herring, bread, and fuel for the fire.

Notes:

January 2
Tuesday

 2nd ♊
☽ → ♋ 10:14 am

Color of the day: Red
Incense of the day: Maple

Blessing Broom Spell

The yuletide season has passed and the traffic in and out of the home has finally slowed down, and now it is time to cleanse your home of old or unwelcome energies and boost protection for those who live there. This can be accomplished in one task. Take a new broom and tie on the following: basil (cleansing), lavender (happiness), nutmeg (good luck), gardenia (peace), cedar (cleansing), lemon slices (cleansing).

Tell the broom that its function is to clean away all residue of the past year and to instill peace, happiness, and good luck for the current year. Sweep the entire house, ending at the back door. Sweep all of the old energy out. Close the door firmly and seal it with a kiss.

Tammy Sullivan

Notes:

January 3
Wednesday

 2nd ♊
Full Moon 8:57 am

Color of the day: Yellow
Incense of the day: Gardenia

Communication Spell

Both the Sun and Mercury are in Capricorn on a Full Moon, creating wonderful conditions for a little magic to ensure that your communications go smoothly and successfully. With this extra boost, you are sure to create success wherever you go today! The secret to the magic is in the breath mints. Get yourself a small box of them in any flavor you like. When you wake up, present the breath mints to each of the cardinal directions and ask for blessings on your communications today. At east, ask for the gifts of clarity and inspiration. At south, ask for the ability to be passionate yet sensitive. At west, ask for guidance that you might act with wisdom instead of reacting with extreme emotion. At north, ask for strength and courage along with the ability to ground intuition into physical communications. Visualize and feel the spirits of each direction filling the mints with these blessings. Give thanks and end your ritual. Use these mints throughout the day, particularly when you need your best communication skills for a challenging situation. Each time you pop one into your mouth, feel the blessings of the spirits fill and guide you.

Kristin Madden

Notes:

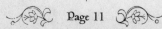

January 4
Thursday

 3rd ♋
)) → ♌ 4:14 pm

Color of the day: Green
Incense of the day: Cedar

Mari Lwyd Spell

In Wales, the season between Yule and Twelfth Night was the time for the ancient procession of the *Mari Lwyd*. A group of men processed from house to house with a decorated horse skull held on a pole. The procession came to the door to engage in a poetic battle of wits with those inside. If the people inside the house could not outwit the Mari Lwyd, the party was let indoors and much chaos ensued. This custom was probably transferred from the Celtic New Year on November 1, the white or grey mare symbolizing the powerful Goddess of Sovereignty who ruled at this time of year. Take time to meditate upon the potent female energy present at the great turning of the wheel, the point of death, darkness, and creation.

Sharynne NicMhacha

Notes:

January 5
Friday

 3rd ♌
Color of the day: White
Incense of the day: Evergreen

Hooray! It's Friday! Spell

For most people who work a Monday through Friday work week, returning home from work on Friday is a mini-celebration. No matter your schedule, you can treat your Friday after-work time as a time to cheer. As you walk through the door to your home, mentally leave your work at the doorway where you can pick it up when you leave again. Change out of the clothes you wore to your job and put on something that you love to wear. Light a candle in your favorite color and put on your favorite music. Light lavender incense for happiness and settle into a relaxed state. Breathe in a sense of relaxation and joy. When you're done, pour yourself your favorite drink and do a silly little happy dance!

Gail Wood

Notes:

January 6
Saturday

3rd ♌

Color of the day: Brown
Incense of the day: Ginger

Overdid It Spell

The holidays are over. You've made it through your first week back at work or school and it's time to contemplate how much you "overdid it." Take some time today to reflect on what you did this past month. Did you put on a few too many pounds? The longer you wait, the harder it will be to get them off and keep them off. Start now. Examine your diet and start eating healthy and exercising regularly. Did you overspend? You don't want to wait for the bills to arrive, because by then it will be too late to plan for them. Review them and put that first payment away now. Think about pacing yourself a bit better this year. Give some consideration to a healthier New Year.

Boudica

Notes:

Holiday lore: Twelfth night and the night following it are when wassailing used to take place. The word "wassail" comes from the Anglo-Saxon words *waes heil*, meaning "to be whole or healthy." People drank to each other's health from a large bowl filled with drink such as "lamb's wool," which was made of hot ale or cider, nutmeg, and sugar with roasted crab apples. In some parts of Britain, trees and bees are still wassailed to ensure a healthy crop. Having drunk to the tree's health, people fire shotguns into the branches. Different regions sing different wassail songs to the tree. Here's one from Worcestershire:

> Here's to thee, old apple tree, Whence thou may-est bud, Whence thou mayest blow, Whence thou mayest bear apples enow.

January 7
Sunday

 3rd ♌
　　　☽ → ♍ 1:18 am

Color of the day: Yellow
Incense of the day: Jasmine

Energizing Spell

Make your exercise routine magical. Don't have a routine? Now is a good time to begin. Choose an activity you enjoy—jogging, weights, yoga—and concentrate on the results you desire. Before you begin each time, center yourself and focus your intent on your goal, whether it's weight loss, muscle toning, or just a feeling of general well-being. The body is a vehicle for the soul and we must care for it to keep it in the best condition. Make your exercise a ritual. Choose music that makes you feel good and raises your energy level. Pay special attention to your breathing. During your warm-up activity, face east and chant the following out loud or silently:

> Power of the radiant Sun,
> Fill me with your glow.
> My body is a special gift,
> Let my strength and
> spirit grow.

> Ember

Notes:

January 8
Monday

 3rd ♍

　　　Color of the day: Lavender
Incense of the day: Cinnamon

Moon-Kissed Hands Spell

Place a consecrated moonstone in a large heatproof bowl or cauldron. Fill the container with pleasantly warm water. Let it sit for three minutes. Remove the stone and add three drops of your favorite essential oil into the cauldron. Stir clockwise thirteen times. Remove adornments from your hands and soak them in the water for thirteen minutes as you meditate.

> Cerridwen Iris Shea

Notes:

January 9
Tuesday

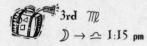 3rd ♏

☽ → ♎ 1:15 pm

Color of the day: White
Incense of the day: Lilac

Winter Car Charm

Use this little car charm to help ward off car problems in what for many of us are the more severe parts of winter. Into a small charm bag place a charged carnelian, a peppermint tea bag, and eighteen mustard seeds. Passing the charm bag over a candle flame, recite the following incantation:

> By all of the powers
> that be
> This car shall be
> kept free
> Of bumps and dings
> And whumps and pings.
> This is my will
> So mote it be!

In your mind, see your car whole and in good working condition. Stash the charm in the glove box to continue its work.

Laurel Reufner

Notes:

January 10
Wednesday

3rd ♎

Color of the day: Brown
Incense of the day: Honeysuckle

Do Nothing Spell

It's time to honor the dormant time and allow yourself to rest before the active growth of new ideas. Here is a "do nothing" spell. Place two unlit green candles in the center of a space. Place a needle and thread and a pair of scissors alongside the candles. Place a small cup of dirt and a packet of seeds on the other side of the candles. Think about the need for all living things to be dormant in order to gather the energy necessary for growth, and remind yourself that you too need that time of rest. Think about the projects you want to start and nurture in the coming year. Now give yourself permission to do nothing about them until you have rested and replenished your energy.

Paniteowl

Notes:

January 11
Thursday

 3rd ♎
4th quarter 7:44 am

Color of the day: Turquoise
Incense of the day: Maple

Ice Magic Spell

One of the greatest natural forces of our planet is ice. It created the valleys and carved the canyons. It freezes the lakes and ponds until they are smooth as glass. Since ice is related to the element of water, it is ideal for spells when you want to cleanse yourself of a bad habit or problem. To use ice in spell work, try this. Write your habit or problem on a small piece of white paper using blue ink. Fold the paper small enough to fit into the cube of an ice cube tray. Add water; freeze the paper. When you feel the time is right, take the ice cube containing your handwritten problem and throw it into a fire. As the ice melts, so will your problem.

James Kambos

Notes:

January 12
Friday

 4th ♎
☽ → ♏ 2:08 am

Color of the day: Pink
Incense of the day: Vanilla

Calling Lares Spell

Today is the festival of Compitalia. This ancient Italian holiday celebrated the Lares—ancestral spirits that protect and preserve family traditions and knowledge. According to tradition, the Lares are associated with the hearth. A small Lare house was constructed by the hearth, daily prayers were spoken there, and offerings of milk, honey, and cakes were left for the spirits. If you'd like to work with the Lares today, try calling them now, on their festival day. Leave out a traditional offering and ask them to bless your hearth, family, and home.

The Lares are the
guardians of the family.

Welcome to my house,
bring peace and security.

On this your festival day,
I do honor the past,

Bless us today, may our
magical traditions last.

Ellen Dugan

January 13
Saturday

 4th ♏

Color of the day: Gray
Incense of the day: Parsley

Banishing Negativity Spell

We've all heard the saying "You are what you eat." In fact, you are what you think. Many of our limitations are set by our thinking patterns or negative self-talk. How many times have you caught yourself saying something like this: "I've never been good at…" "They will never listen to me…" "I can't do that…" Harness the power of the waning Moon tonight to banish or reduce limiting and negative thought patterns. On a dark-colored piece of paper, write any doubts you have about your potential. Imagine the paper absorbing the ink, overpowering the words. Tear the paper into tiny pieces and place in a sieve. Burn the paper over a candle flame until it burns to ash while you say:

> Paper of limitations,
> As you burn to dust
> while torn,
> Banish my negative
> thinking
> As my true potential is
> born.

Discard the ash outside or flush it down the toilet.

Emely Flak

Notes:

January 14
Sunday

 4th ♏

☽ → ♐ 1:11 pm

Color of the day: Orange
Incense of the day: Violet

Wholeness Spell

This is a time to honor the rational and logical mind and the instinctual, natural parts of ourselves. Wholeness is key here. You need two pieces of string nine inches, feet, or yards long. Use light blue, yellow, or gold to represent your logical, thinking side. For your instinctive side, use colors such as red and brown. In front of your altar or during a ritual, take both strands together. You'll be making nine knots. Before tying each knot, say:

> Heart and head
> combined as one,
> Ruled both by Moon and
> by Sun.
> I unite both inside me.
> For the good of all, so
> mote it be.

Keep the string in a safe place. When you feel the need to repeat the spell, run your fingers over each knot and repeat the chant.

Olivia O'Meir

Notes:

January 15
Monday

Martin Luther King, Jr. Day

 4th ♐

Color of the day: White
Incense of the day: Coriander

Spaghetti Spell

Spaghetti contains all of the necessary ingredients to banish negativity and instill protection, love, and healing in those who consume it. Tomatoes promote love and protection; basil promotes love, protection, and banishes negativity; garlic promotes love, protection, and healing and also banishes negativity. These three ingredients are central to any spaghetti recipe. As you combine the ingredients of your favorite recipe, charge the food with energy. Hold each ingredient in your hand and say:

It is my will that you release your magical vibrations of love, healing, and protection as well as flavor. Banish all negative thoughts and feelings. Those who partake shall be blessed by this food. It is my will that this food harmonize the mind, body, and soul. Make it so!

Tammy Sullivan

Notes:

January 16
Tuesday

4th ♐
☽ → ♑ 8:49 pm

Color of the day: Black
Incense of the day: Coriander

Bad Habits Fire Spell

The January waning Moon is an excellent time to rid yourself of bad habits. Use this day, the festival of the Buddhist fire god Betoro Bromo, to transform your bad habits into more positive practices. Center a red candle in a cauldron filled one-quarter full of sand. Gather objects that represent your bad habits, or if that's not possible, write them on slips of paper. Prepare an offering to the gods of fire. Basil, clove, and frankincense are excellent choices as these are herbs used in exorcisms and are aligned with fire energies. Light the candle, and as you gaze at the flame let the mundane slip from your thoughts. Begin by sprinkling your herbal offering into the flame. Ask the fire gods to assist you in your spell. Hold the objects that represent your bad habits in your passive hand. Thank them for serving you. Kiss them and release them into the flame.

Lily Gardner

Notes:

January 17
Wednesday

 4th ♑

Color of the day: Topaz
Incense of the day: Poplar

Dark Moon Meditation

*T*oday is Benjamin Franklin's birthday, and one of the well-known folk stories about him is his discovery that lightning is electricity. He tied a key to a kite and flew it in a storm, and when lightning struck the kite the key gave off an electric shock. Keys are a potent symbol of freedom and discovery. They open doorways. By the dark of the Moon, you can reflect on the keys to discovery in your own life. Settle down into your darkened meditative space with a key in your closed fist. Breathe deeply and fully. Keep on breathing, and ask the spirits to give you insights about what keys and discovery mean to you. Then open your hand, hold the key outward, and ask, "What doorways does this open for me?" Wait for the answer that will surely come to you. Breathe deeply, thank the spirits, and move into discovery.

Gail Wood

Notes:

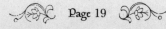

January 18
Thursday

 4th ♑

New Moon 11:01 pm

Color of the day: Purple
Incense of the day: Pine

Offering to the Hag Spell

In Scottish tradition, winter was the seasonal domain of the *Cailleach* or Hag. She was an ancient figure who helped create the landscape, carrying mountains and boulders in her apron that shaped the land wherever they fell. She lived in a cave filled with the bones of oxen, as numerous as the many years she has existed. Her name means "The Veiled One," and she was a powerful divine figure who presided over the fertility and abundance of the wilderness, herding flocks of wild deer and guarding springs and wells. Make an offering to the Cailleach by pouring mead or cream on a holed stone, saying:

> Veiled One, Old One,
> Mother of Snow
> Who stirs the cauldron
> of the waters below,
> I honor you and pour on stone
> This offering to the dark of bone.

Sharynne NicMhacha

Notes:

January 19
Friday

 1st ♑

☽ → ♒ 1:15 am

Color of the day: Rose
Incense of the day: Sandalwood

Husband's Day Love Spell

There is nothing like a cold January night to make you appreciate your mate. Use this time-honored charm to deepen love and promote passion in your relationship. This is not a coercive spell, but rather a charm that works on your own emotions. As you prepare this charm, feel yourself deeply appreciating your partner. Place two sewing needles side by side so that the point of one needle lines up with the eye of the other. Wrap the needles in a newly picked leaf (a leaf from a houseplant will do). Tie the packet with a red ribbon or red yarn twice—two being the number of partnership. Now insert the charm in a red cloth bag and center the bag under your bed. As long as the charm remains under the bed, undisturbed, it will continue to work.

Lily Gardner

Notes:

away on frivolous pursuits? Do we make time for ourselves? Take time to make time for those things that really matter to yourself and to your family.

Boudica

Notes:

January 20
Saturday
Islamic New Year

 1st ♒

☉ → ♒ 6:01 am

Color of the day: Blue
Incense of the day: Coriander

Passage of Time Spell

While this date is noted on the Islamic calendar, it is not an official holiday and is not celebrated. It is, according to tradition, a date used to mark the passage of time. Time: it's something we all wish we had more of, yet we squander it so readily. Time does not stand still, nor can we collect it and save it for when we really need it. Take time today to reflect on how you use your own time. Do you spend enough time with your family? Are we making the most of our time? Do we fill each day with meaningful and prosperous jobs and ideas, or do we waste the days

January 21
Sunday

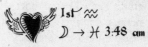 1st ♒

☽ → ♓ 3:48 am

Color of the day: Gold
Incense of the day: Cedar

Saint Agnes Day Dream Spell

Saint Agnes was a Roman virgin martyr and the patron saint of girls. She was prayed to by young women who hoped to learn the identity of their future mates. This was done by using the herbs which are sacred to her—rosemary and thyme. Just before bedtime tonight, scent your bedroom with rosemary and thyme by burning them, or stuff a sprig of each into a dream pillow. Upon falling asleep, think of your intent while saying softly: "Saint Agnes gentle and kind, let me see my lover in my mind." According to tradition, you'll not only dream of your future lover, but you'll also hear him whisper words of love.

James Kambos

Notes:

Holiday lore: Feast Day of Saint Agnes of Rome. Since the fourth century, the primitive church held Saint Agnes in high honor above all the other virgin martyrs of Rome. Church fathers and Christian poets sang her praises, and they extolled her virginity and heroism under torture. The feast day for Saint Agnes was assigned to January 21. Early records gave the same date for her feast, and the Catholic Church continues to keep her memory sacred.

January 22
Monday

1st ♓

Color of the day: Silver
Incense of the day: Basil

Protection Spell

Today is the feast day of Saint Vincent, patron saint of wine and vinegar makers. To dispel negativity in yourself and others, on this morning fill a jar with a cup of cider vinegar and a tablespoon of sea salt. Cover and set the jar in a window to absorb the Sun's protective energies. At night, prepare a bath in which you add the Sun-enhanced vinegar solution. Burn four white candles in the four directions surrounding your tub. Allow yourself to soak for at least twenty minutes, visualizing yourself freed from feelings of fear, fatigue, depression, and self-criticism, and protected from others' negativity. Allow yourself to air-dry to maintain this fine membrane of protection.

> Remember on Saint
> Vincent's Day
> If that the Sun his
> beams display.
> For 'tis a token, bright
> and clear
> Of prosperous weather
> all the year.

Lily Gardner

 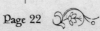

Notes:

And stumbles and fear.
Clear as water flows,
Feet follow, heart goes.
Clean as the path lies,
Ice melts and doubt dies.

You may recast this spell as needed whenever you shovel snow or spread rock salt outside.

Elizabeth Barrette

Notes:

January 23
Tuesday

1st ♓
☽ → ♈ 5:52 am

Color of the day: Gray
Incense of the day: Myrrh

Safe Footing Spell

The element of water flows through our lives, tempering our emotions and granting us intuition. In winter, though, water can turn treacherous—and sometimes emotions can seem as slippery as an icy sidewalk! Here is a dual-purpose spell to facilitate safe footing in both the physical and metaphysical realms. Begin by shoveling off your porch, patio, sidewalk, etc. Next you need a container of rock salt (or other salt-based ice inhibitor). Bless the salt by saying, "I charge this salt to work my will. Blessed be!" As you sprinkle it over the ground, say:

Let the path stay clean,
Let the path stay clear.
Banish confusion

January 24
Wednesday

1st ♈

Color of the day: White
Incense of the day: Juniper

Spicy Spell for Success

Mix the following ingredients with mortar and pestle:

3 pinches of dried marjoram
dash of ground cinnamon
dash of ground ginger

Marjoram is ruled by the air element, the spices by fire. Think of the heat of the spices bringing energy to the intellectual element of air, stimulating success. As you combine the

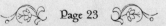

ingredients, visualize the success you wish to achieve. These three herbs are also often used in love spells, so be careful what you wish for success with. In a place where you seek success (home, business, school), sprinkle tiny portions of this mixture in the area. Chant:

> Herbs of air, herbs of fire,
> Bring success that I
> desire.
> Bless this space, herbs of
> three,
> For good of all, so mote
> it be.

Ember

Notes:

To bridge ancient traditions with a busy, modern lifestyle, one also needs a healthy sense of humor and an open mind. One whimsical example of this is the attention gained by an emerging new goddess: Caffeina. Although Caffeina doesn't reside in history books or in our ancient memories or archetypes, she is with us every day, as the prolific consumption of coffee is an integral part of western society. Drinking coffee in its many flavors and manifestations is now woven into the social fabric of our lives. Caffeina teaches us that moderation is the key to enjoying her gift of coffee. Imagine Caffeina as a beautiful woman rising with the steam of your cup. Enjoy a cup of coffee either alone or with friends, and visualize the creativity and energy that Caffeina brings as you drink her nectar.

Emely Flak

Notes:

January 25
Thursday

1st ♈
☽ → ♉ 8:28 am
2nd quarter 6:01 pm

Color of the day: Crimson
Incense of the day: Neroli

New Goddess Spell
Our contemporary Pagan path is a blend of the old and the new.

Holiday lore: Burns' Night is a key event in Scotland that has been observed for about 200 years in honor of Robert Burns, who was born on this day. One of Scotland's most beloved bards, Burns immortalized haggis in a famous poem. This a Scottish dish of animal organs boiled in a sheep's stomach with suet and oatmeal. "Burns' Suppers" are celebrated not only in Scotland but wherever patriotic Scots or those of Scottish descent live.

January 26
Friday

2nd ♉

Color of the day: Coral
Incense of the day: Carnation

Chocolate Love Spell

Strengthen those ties between you and your lover with this delicious spell. Splurge for this spell and buy the best hot chocolate you can afford. You will also need some rose water and two amethyst stones. Candles are nice as well. Make a cup of the decadent hot chocolate for each of you, adding a tablespoon of rose water and an amethyst to each cup. Now snuggle up together, just the two of you, and enjoy your chocolate. Afterward, wash the amethysts and each of you carry one as

a reminder of your relationship and love for one another.

Laurel Reufner

Notes:

January 27
Saturday

2nd ♉

☽ → ♊ 12:10 pm

Color of the day: Indigo
Incense of the day: Dill

Home Protection Ritual

Let's clean house! Gather one white candle in a holder, a stick of sandalwood or patchouli incense, a censer, a cup of water, and a small dish of salt. Set up your supplies in the heart of your home. Light the candle and the incense stick. Mix a pinch of salt into the cup of water and swirl the liquid with your fingers. As you work your way through the house, sprinkle a few drops of water in the corners of the rooms and then wave some of the scented smoke around. Visualize this elemental energy radiating out with protection and positive energy. Repeat this charm as you go:

From the heart of my
home this protection
spell is spun,
Negativity will depart
as my charm is sung.
This home is now blessed
by my will and desire,
I close this spell by earth,
air, water, and fire.

Ellen Dugan

Notes:

day. Now visualize yourself. Placing
a drop of oil on a cotton ball or tissue, breathe in the aroma and imagine this healing energy filling your
entire energy field. Place the cotton
in a plastic bag and carry it with you
today, breathing in the healing scents
whenever you have need.

Kristin Madden

Notes:

January 28
Sunday

2nd ♊

Color of the day: Amber
Incense of the day: Patchouli

healing Scents Spell

Take a moment to be fully present with the essential oils of
fresh rosemary or carnation. Thank
the oils for their healing energies
and ask that they bless your day.
Visualize your home and feel where
there is a need for peace or healing.
In each of these areas, place a drop of
oil on a cotton ball or tissue. Breathe
in the aroma and imagine the energy
of peace and healing filling this space.
Then leave it in the room for the

January 29
Monday

2nd ♊
☽ → ♋ 5:16 pm

Color of the day: Ivory
Incense of the day: Coriander

Protective Eye Charm

Protection magic has been
with us since the beginning
of time. We have sought protection
from the harshness of the natural
elements, the wrath of gods and goddesses, and, unfortunately, from envy
and ill intent from fellow humans.
Throughout history in art and
sculpture, protection often appears
using the symbol of the eye. The
ancient Egyptians used the Eye of

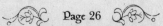

Horus to ward off negativity. In the Mediterranean, an eye charm or amulet is a popular form of protection against the "evil eye." The evil eye, or *malocchio*, as it is called in Italy, is curse directed at you by another person, usually driven by emotions of fear, malice, or jealousy. Victims of the evil eye experience illness and bad luck. You can make your own protective eye charm by painting an eye on a rock or stone. Keep it with you or in your car or desk drawer for protection and imagine it keeping you from harm.

Emely Flak

Notes:

January 30
Tuesday

2nd ♋

Color of the day: Maroon
Incense of the day: Chrysanthemum

Poet for a Day Spell

Poetry is an innate part of our natural rhythm. Song lyrics are poems. Our heartbeat sets an internal rhythm. Our speech patterns form pentameters used in poetry. Seek poetry out today in honor of your natural rhythms and the more universal one. Buy a book of poetry or get one out of the library. Attend a poetry reading. Craft a poem yourself, even if it's only for yourself and your muse. Celebrate your natural poetic rhythm. Today you are a poet. Make your offerings to yourself and to Calliope, the muse of epic poetry.

Cerridwen Iris Shea

Notes:

January 31
Wednesday

2nd ♋

Color of the day: Yellow
Incense of the day: Poplar

Smell the Flowers Spell

In the doldrums of winter, people may get short-tempered and out of sorts. Even those who are not attuned to the Earth's energies are influenced by the cycles of the seasons and may not realize why they are feeling stressed. You, as a magical practitioner, can help others be grounded and centered. Whether going to work, or school, or just meeting friends, bring some flowers with you. Select bright golden colors.

 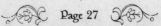

As you arrange the flowers, say:

> Above as below,
> Within as without,
> Cast your beauty thrice
> about.
> Let my wish of love and
> kindness
> Be the spark that will
> remind us.

Then think of all the people who may stop to smell the flowers, or smile at their cheerfulness, and for a moment take that beauty into themselves. Give this gift freely!

Paniteowl

Notes:

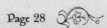

February is the second month of the Gregorian calendar and the year's shortest month. It is named for Februa, an ancient purification festival, and its astrological sign is Aquarius, the water-bearer (January 20–February 18), a fixed air sign ruled by Uranus. In February, Mother Earth begins to stir; daylight lasts a little longer, and the first crocuses begin to peek through the snow. The major holiday of the month, Imbolc or Candlemas, celebrates the strengthening Sun. This is a day of purification and banishment; candles are lit and Yuletide greenery is burned in a ritual fire to illuminate the waning darkness of winter. Corn dollies, called Corn Maidens, are dressed in scraps of white lace and ribbons. The maiden is placed in a basket, called the Bride's Bed, with a small ribbon-entwined wand representing the God. Romance is celebrated on Valentine's Day, February 14. Magical activities include love divinations of all types, and, of course, treating your romantic partner to chocolates is a common custom. Long ago, February's Full Moon was called the Snow Moon, and the month is still known for powerful snowstorms. Still, nature begins to sense the turning of the year. House finches begin looking for nesting sites, and in the still-frozen woodland foxes begin searching for a mate.

February 1
Thursday

 2nd ♋
☽ → ♌ 12:14 am

Color of the day: White
Incense of the day: Sandalwood

Cabin Fever Spell

Winter drives our thoughts inward as the harsh weather makes it inconvenient or impossible to travel or work outside. Introspection has its place, but after a while cabin fever starts to set in. At this time of year, it's good to get together with a few friends. Throughout history, Europeans and Americans have held "salons"—social gatherings that center around discussing a particular topic. The Inuit have "potlatches" where people share food and gifts. In Ireland, women celebrate February 1 as Wives' Day. They hold lavish celebrations of their skills as homemakers by cooking beautiful feasts for each other. So pick a topic important to you—maybe something magical or spiritual. Write out invitations on elegant cards and gather some friends for an evening of intelligent conversation. Devote a day to cooking those extraordinary recipes that taste oh-so-good but take hours to make. You deserve it!

Elizabeth Barrette

Notes:

February 2
Friday
Imbolc – Groundhog Day

 2nd ♌
Full Moon 12:45 am

Color of the day: Purple
Incense of the day: Sandalwood

Nature Meditation Ritual

Even though it may still feel like winter, life is stirring in the earth. Use this special day to honor the elements and get in touch with nature. Since the Moon is full tonight, try to perform this ritual near a window where the moonlight can shine through, or outdoors if weather permits. You will need a stone of your choice (and/or a handful of clean soil), a leaf, a feather, a container of water, and a candle. Light the candle and place it in front of you (or in the center of a group ritual). Touch each item mindfully and consider how each one represents an element: earth, air, fire, and water. Hold the stone or leaf in your hands, dip your fingers in the water, stroke the feather, gaze upon the candle flame. Consider how vital each element is to life. As you consider each element, use the following chant:

> Field, flower, tree, and stone;
> Build the Earth that I call home.
> Changing wind, air to breathe,
> Precious atmosphere and breeze.
> Candle flame, fire bright,
> Warmth and heat, radiant light.
> Drink of life in flow or freeze,
> Rain and river, spring and sea.

Ember

Notes:

Holiday lore: On Imbolc, a bundle of corn from the harvest is dressed in ribbons and becomes the Corn Bride. On February 2, the Corn Bride is placed on the hearth or hung on the door to bring prosperity, fertility, and protection to the home.

February 3
Saturday

 3rd ♌
☽ → ♍ 9:34 am

Color of the day: Brown
Incense of the day: Thyme

Love Oil Spell

The Imbolc season, which was a time of rebirth and renewed abundance, may also have been a sacred ritual period of purification in preparation for the renewed energies of spring. Various sacred plants were used throughout the winter season for this purpose. In Scotland, juniper was burned at the New Year to *sain* or purify the home. *Torannon*, or figwort, was utilized around Imbolc for protection and abundance. The dandelion was sacred to Bridget, and its root is still used for purification. In Scotland great fires of gorse were made, and the herb called "broom" was burned as well. Prepare a ritual incense for purification and protection in preparation for spring. Mix together juniper, dandelion root, broom, and figwort, and use the smoke to smudge your home and your loved ones.

Sharynne NicMhacha

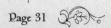

February 4
Sunday

3rd ♏

Color of the day: Orange
Incense of the day: Lilac

Visualization for a Better World

Light your favorite incense and a lovely candle. Play soft music. Close your eyes and come to center, breathing deeply. Once you are calm and relaxed, imagine the world the way you wish it to be. Take your time, filling it with rich detail, love and joy. Use as much love and positive emotion as you can to fill your vision. Chant "peace, beauty, love" as your mantra during the visualization. Revisit this meditation once a week, and start putting into practice the life you envision.

Cerridwen Iris Shea

Notes:

February 5
Monday

3rd ♏
☽ → ♎ 9:15 pm

Color of the day: Gray
Incense of the day: Clove

Silver Coin Divination

According to legend, this is a powerful day for divination. Since this is a day ruled by the Moon, the following divination would be appropriate. Fill a cauldron or a dark-colored bowl with water. Drop a silver coin into the water and darken the room. Light a candle behind you. When the surface of the water is still, gaze intently at the coin. Blink naturally and relax. The water-filled cauldron represents the depths of the inner self. The coin signifies the Moon in its full phase, and the height of psychic power. Think of a specific question. Your answer may come to you as a symbol or an actual image. The water may mist over and then clear, revealing an image. Keep your scrying sessions short—about ten minutes. If you wish, keep a journal of the things you see.

James Kambos

Notes:

February 6
Tuesday

3rd ♎

Color of the day: Red
Incense of the day: Daffodil

Rekindling Spell

February is time to rekindle the flame for those of us who have already found the love of our lives. Letting that special someone know that you are still in love can be very rewarding for both of you. From your photo albums, make a collage of your loved one. Let the photos remind you of who this person is as an individual. As you assemble the collage, picture the two of you as you grow old together. Add whatever you like to the arrangement. When the collage is finished, take a needle and thread and stitch around the collage, chanting:

> A stitch in time,
> A step in time.
> I'm so glad
> That you are mine.

Put the finished collage in a place where your loved one will see it and know that you have been thinking of him or her.

Paniteowl

Notes:

February 7
Wednesday

3rd ♎

Color of the day: White
Incense of the day: Evergreen

Banish Workday Blues Spell

February is famous for cold, dreary weather that saps energy and makes the mind numb. This spell heats our productivity back up and releases the workday blues. Build a small fire in your cauldron. Write down each symptom on separate slips of paper—for instance, "low energy" or "weariness." As you write the words, channel that emotion through your arm and onto the paper. Throw them into the fire and say:

> Begone all feelings of
> boredom and blues.
> It is the glow of joy I
> choose.
> No longer will my day be
> too much for me;
> I spend my time
> productively.

 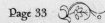

I am happy with high
energy.
As I speak it, so mote
it be!

Sprinkle blessed salt over the ashes
and scatter them to the winds.

Tammy Sullivan

Notes:

strikes you as perfect, a few gold or
yellow candles lit for the opportunity
can only help. Local newspapers offer
daily job opportunities. Network
with friends and former workmates.
A positive attitude will help you find
that perfect job.

Boudica

Notes:

February 8
Thursday

 3rd ♎
☽ → ♏ 10:09 am

Color of the day: Crimson
Incense of the day: Coriander

Job hunting Spell

The best time to acquire a new
job is in the first three months
of the year, when you will find more
opportunities and most likely be
hired. If you are job hunting, examine
your resume, polish it, and get help
if you feel it is not up to standard.
There are many websites that offer
advice on resumes, and there are
books available from the library as
well. Draw a pentacle with your
finger on the resumes you send out.
It will bring you luck. And if a job

Holiday lore: Today is the Buddhist
Needle Memorial. On this
day, as part of the principle of endless compassion espoused by the
Buddhist faith for all sentient and
nonsentient beings, all the sewing
needles that have been retired during
the year are honored. That is, needles
are brought to the shrine and pushed
into a slab of tofu that rests on the
second tier of a three-tiered altar.
Priests sing sutras to comfort the needles and heal their injured spirits.

February 9
Friday

 3rd ♏

Color of the day: Rose
Incense of the day: Geranium

Lovin' Feelings Spell

Venus, Mercury, and the Moon are all in watery, emotional planets today. This is a day for love and good feelings. And what better way to do this than simply spray it on? To make the Lovin' Spray, add eight to ten drops of the essential oils of rose and vanilla to half a cup of distilled water in a spray bottle. (If you want to keep this spray for several months, use a dark glass bottle with a spray top.) Screw the top on tightly. Invert the bottle three times to mix the ingredients as you ask the energies of rose and vanilla to fill this water with happiness and love. Spray this on first thing in the morning and take a moment to experience the good feelings it gives you. Then take it with you for a little pick-me-up throughout the day . . . or share it with others.

Kristin Madden

Notes:

February 10
Saturday

 3rd ♏
4th quarter 4:51 am
☽ → ♐ 10:01 pm

Color of the day: Blue
Incense of the day: Sandalwood

Outside the Box Spell

Sometimes you need to be able to think outside the box a little. This spell produces a charmed stone you can carry with you and use when needed. Before performing the spell, you will need to find the right stone to use. The only essential requirement is that it feels comfortable in your hand. Other than that it can be any stone. Cleanse the stone under running water and cup it in your hand. Pour your will into the stone and visualize your problems disappearing. Set the stone in the moonlight for the night. After that, carry it with you, and when you need a creative solution to some problem, take it out and worry it while you think.

Laurel Reufner

Notes:

February 11
Sunday

 4th ♐

Color of the day: Amber
Incense of the day: Juniper

Sunday Spell

This is the day of the Lady of Lourdes. Why not take a moment and celebrate what is, in essence, another amazing aspect of the Mother Goddess? This Sunday spell calls in the powers of the Sun and the Mother Goddess to promote success and good health. Set up on your working space one white and one blue candle, each in its holder. Add two yellow rosebuds for hope, happiness, and the energies of the Sun. Then light the candles and repeat the charm:

> Yellow roses do promote
> joy and happiness,
>
> Call on the great
> Mother, and your spell
> she will bless.
>
> On this day that belongs
> to the bright golden Sun,
>
> Send to me success and
> health, and bring harm
> to none.

Ellen Dugan

February 12
Monday

 4th ♐

Color of the day: Lavender
Incense of the day: Poplar

Find a Penny Spell

Today is Abraham Lincoln's birthday, and his face graces the American penny. This is also "Lost Penny Day," a day to find pennies and circulate these coins back into the economy. Pennies seem to have little value, but they are the cornerstone of many monetary systems. The old rhyme "Find a penny and pick it up, all day long you'll have good luck" is truly a spell of continuing power. Luck seems so elusive, but it can be as common as a penny. Gather pennies from the stray places throughout your home. As you pick each one up, chant:

> I found this penny and
> picked it up. All day long
> I'll have good luck.

Place the pennies in a bowl on your altar. Whenever you need luck, take

 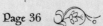

a blessed penny and carry it through the day. When the day is over, donate the penny to a good cause.

Gail Wood

Notes:

February 13
Tuesday

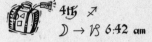

4th ♐
☽ → ♑ 6:42 am

Color of the day: White
Incense of the day: Rose

Parentalia Ritual

The ancient Romans honored Parentalia, a nine-day festival that commenced on this day to remember one's dead parents. During this time, families visited tombs to make offerings of food, flowers, or wine. Sometimes, and sadly, when someone we love passes away we take little time to grieve and heal. We wish we shared more time together or told them that we cherished them. This is particularly true for parents. When they depart, we may feel guilt for our lack of appreciation. These feelings retard the grieving process. To help the healing, find an item that the person wore in contact with his or her skin, like jewelry or a small piece of clothing. Light a small candle in a bowl. Write down something you wish you had communicated to that person. Burn the paper with your written message in the flame and imagine the words being delivered to your loved one. Keep the personal memento close to you, either in your purse or on your person, until you feel the healing begin.

Emely Flak

Holiday lore: Lincoln is called the Great Emancipator and is thought of as one of our greatest presidents. Know this, however: Lincoln was an almost unknown figure until the age of forty, when he first entered the Illinois state legislature. His later assassination threw the country into widespread mourning, inspiring Walt Whitman to write:

Coffin that passes
through lanes and street,
through day and night
with the great cloud
darkening the land . . .
I mourned, and yet shall
mourn with ever—
returning spring.

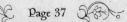
Page 37

Notes:

loved ones, and prepare it with love. Eat by candlelight. Send loving e-mails or postcards to friends and family. Appreciate inspiration, inspire others, and grow love in the coming season.

Cerridwen Iris Shea

Notes:

February 14
Wednesday
Valentine's Day

4th ♑

Color of the day: Brown
Incense of the day: Sage

Love and Light Spell

February 14 has become a night of forced and unromantic romance. This year, take it back and make it yours. Today in 1824, *Ladies' Garland*, the first newspaper addressing the interests of women, was published in the U.S. Today in 1912, Arizona became the forty-eighth state. It's the eve of Lupercalia, the Roman festival of the she-wolf, a day of purification and fertility. It was also the "Old Candlemass" in many traditions, before Candlemass was realigned to February 2. Celebrate who and what you love in this life. Use beautiful scented candles to illuminate your home. Surround yourself with sensual, textural foods, clothing, and experiences. Prepare a meal with your

February 15
Thursday

4th ♑
☽ → ♒ 11:34 am

Color of the day: Turquoise
Incense of the day: Eucalyptus

Silencing Your Inner Critic

Our inner critic can be our harshest judge. It is different from our instinct or our inner editor, since they seek to protect and improve us. The inner critic seeks to take advantage of us and our fears. Before this spell, think about what shape the critic would be. Would it be a person? How about a symbol or mythological figure? What colors would it be? When ready, take a piece of parchment and pen. Now draw your inner critic on it. Next, light it on fire and place it in a heat-proof container. While it is burning, say:

Inner critic gone away,
Not to return another day.
Now my soul is free
To take opportunities in
front of me.
For the good of all,
So mote it be.

Olivia O'Meir

Notes:

the burning paper in the cauldron,
and as it burns, imagine everything
you don't like about yourself melting
away. All your positive qualities will
take the place of the negative. You are
beautiful.

Ember

Notes:

February 16
Friday

4♄ ≈

Color of the day: Coral
Incense of the day: Musk

Confidence Spell

"Love thyself" is a popular
mantra. But the key to relationships is first being confident and
loving who you are. Light a green
candle and situate yourself in front of
a mirror. Look at your reflection. See
within as well as without. On a sheet
of paper, make two lists: things you
like about yourself and things you
don't. You are the only person who
will ever see this, so be honest. Then
tear off the part of the paper where
you've listed negative qualities and
light it with the candle flame. Place

February 17
Saturday

4♄ ≈
New Moon 11:14 am
☽ → ♓ 1:30 pm

Color of the day: Indigo
Incense of the day: Ylang-ylang

Destruction and Renewal Spell

Today is the birthday of Kali. As
the Hindu goddess of destruction, Kali is often feared. However,
with her force she reminds us that
after destruction comes renewal.
Such are the cycles of life. Instead
of worrying about her fierce, relent-
less energies, honor her courage to
dismantle structures that no longer
serve a purpose and make way for
new beginnings. Ask for Kali's
strength to end a cycle in your life

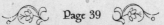

that needs closure or letting go, or to invoke fortitude when you wish to commence a new project. With change comes the challenge of leaving your comfort zone. Here is a short spell to ask for the guidance of Kali through change:

> What I am going through
> Feels foreign and strange.
> Kali, I invite your energy
> To help me manage this
> change.

Emely Flak

Notes:

invite friends in for dinner and order take-out, or show off your own gourmet skills by preparing a variety of Chinese dishes to share. This is a day to celebrate the ancestors, for they are the foundation of our lives. It is also a day to show our friends and relatives how important they are to us. Have a sheet of paper for each of your guests, and don't forget yourself. Have each person write his or her name on one of the sheets and then pass them around, asking everyone to write a wish or make a loving comment about the person whose name is on the paper. What you are doing is trading spells of love and support. Enjoy the day!

Paniteowl

Notes:

February 18
Sunday

Chinese New Year (boar)

 1st ♓
☉ → ♓ 8:09 pm

Color of the day: Gold
Incense of the day: Frankincense

Chinese New Year Spell

Today, celebrate with family and friends. Borrow some of the traditions of the Chinese New Year celebrations: fill your home with colorful floral arrangements,

February 19
Monday

 1st ♓
☽ → ♈ 2:06 pm

Color of the day: White
Incense of the day: Frankincense

Banish the Blahs Spell

Use the energy of the New Moon to banish prevailing doldrums within your household. You'll need to gather some soft pillows beforehand and place them about your main family room. Take a moment to take several deep breaths and ground yourself a bit. Go into the main family room, put on some fun music, and throw a pillow at another family member, starting a grand pillow fight. If you live by yourself, put on the music and dance around. Afterward, watch a favorite movie together and enjoy some popcorn. Repeat as needed.

Laurel Reufner

Notes:

February 20
Tuesday

Mardi Gras

 1st ♈

Color of the day: Maroon
Incense of the day: Frankincense

Mardi Gras Ritual

This is a day of festivals and fun before Ash Wednesday, the beginning of Lent. Also known as Shrove Tuesday, it is a day of confession. To observe this day, burn a light sweet copal incense and announce what you wish to change in your life. Decorate your altar with colorful cloth, ribbons, beads, or glitter. If you wish, invite friends in and let them wear masks or other finery. Serve wine and appetizers. As the day winds down and after guests have left, run a bath. Sprinkle the water with sea salt. Bathe as usual, allowing the bath to serve as a form of spiritual cleansing. Spend the days leading up to Ostara performing good works and clearing away the spiritual clutter in your life.

James Kambos

Notes:

February 21
Wednesday

Ash Wednesday

 1st ♈

☽ → ♉ 3:03 pm

Color of the day: Yellow
Incense of the day: Frankincense

hangover Spell

On this day after Mardi Gras, a spell to banish a hangover seems like just the ticket. Drink lots of water to help purify your system, and call on the god Hermes. Ask that he impart a little of his healing energy swiftly to you. Gather together a small purple candle and coordinating candle holder, and some of the trinkets from the celebrations—beads, a mask, etc. Arrange these around your purple candle. Repeat the spell three times. Allow the candle to burn out in a safe place on its own.

> May the god hermes
> hear my request.
>
> Wave your caduceus my
> way, so I can heal and
> rest.
>
> Send healing swiftly
> to me, I overdid it last
> night,
>
> Banish this hangover,
> so I can get on with my
> life.

Ellen Dugan

Notes:

February 22
Thursday

 1st ♉

Color of the day: Green
Incense of the day: Cedar

harmony Spell

On this day, the ancient Romans celebrated Concordia, also known as Caristia. They recognized the importance of harmony among family and friends. Each family would hold a feast and do their best to mend any quarrels among themselves. They exchanged small gifts and reconnected with loved ones. In music, harmony results from the concord of two or more different sounds. Without both the difference and the concord, there could be no harmony; and the same is true of human relationships. Celebrate today by sharing favorite family songs with

your loved ones. You might begin
with a chant such as this:

> We are simply notes
> In a larger song
> All our doubts and hopes
> Carry us along
>
> Voices in a chord
> Souls in symphony
> Weaving long and short
> Perfect harmony

Elizabeth Barrette

Notes:

Holiday lore: We all know the
lore about our first president—
cherry tree, silver dollar, wooden
teeth—but the truth behind this most
legendary of American figures is
sometimes more entertaining than
the folklore. For instance, did you
know that once when young George
went for a dip in the Rappahannock
River, two Fredericksburg women stole
his clothes? This story was recorded in
the Spotsylvania County records.
Picture then the young man scamper-
ing home flustered and naked, and the
icon of the dollar bill becomes just a bit
more real.

February 23
Friday

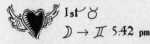 1st ♉

☽ → ♊ 5:42 pm

Color of the day: Pink
Incense of the day: Sandalwood

Keep Love Alive Spell

While the traditional romantic
day of Valentine's Day has
come and gone, this herbal bath
keeps that special feeling alive year
round. Draw a warm bath and add
the following herbs by the handful:
red rose petals, jasmine petals, and
lavender flowers. Add a pinch of cinnamon and throw in a rose-quartz
crystal and blessed salt. Light two
pink candles. Place your right index
finger in the water and channel
romantic, sexy vibrations all through
it. Water is a fantastic conductor for
energy. Say,

> I call into the universe
> to express and enforce
> my will.
>
> I call love unto me,
> I call romance unto me,
> I call happiness and
> passion unto me.
> I call harmony and
> balance unto me.
>
> My Lord and Lady,
> as I am you and you are
> me,

for now and all time,
these things will be!

Tammy Sullivan

Notes:

From January to
December, I will
remember.

Breathe the scents in deeply as you chant. Whenever you put on this jewelry (and even when you don't wear it), chant:

I remember what I need
to know. As I will it,
make it so.

Gail Wood

Notes:

February 24
Saturday

1st ♊
2nd Quarter 2:56 am

Color of the day: Gray
Incense of the day: Nutmeg

Conquering CRS Spell

"I have CRS: Can't Remember Stuff," you say. Folklore says that a string around the finger reminds us of what we need to know. These kinds of memory aids work wonders. To create a memory aid, gather together some dried rosemary and cloves, patchouli incense, and a piece of jewelry that you wear often. Rings are especially effective because they are reminiscent of the string on the finger. Place the jewelry in a small bowl with the rosemary and cloves. Light the incense and pass it over the bowl, chanting three times:

February 25
Sunday

2nd ♊
☽ → ♋ 10:47 pm

Color of the day: Yellow
Incense of the day: Lavender

Sun Light Tea

Bring the healthy, revitalizing energies of the Sun into your life today through a delicious tea. If you live in an area of the world that is experiencing summer at this time of year, feel free to ice your tea as a cool escape from the heat. But a warm cup of tea will certainly contribute to your experience of the

Sun's energy. Pour boiling water over a chamomile tea bag and a cinnamon stick. As you dissolve half a teaspoon of local honey in the hot water, imagine the brilliant, life-giving light of the Sun in the center of your tea cup. Stirring clockwise, see this light spread and fill the tea to overflowing. Allow the tea to steep for nine minutes before removing the tea bag and stick. With each sip, feel the warm light of the Sun spread throughout your body.

Kristin Madden

Notes:

standard bulbs. Fresh flowers or even artificial ones can add a springlike feeling. Floral scents such as lavender or lilac will make the house smell like spring. Wash curtains, bed linens, and towels with a fabric softener that has that "spring fresh" scent. Add a new picture that brings spring to mind, or paint one. Maybe add some new, brighter colors around the house to help lift the winter doldrums. Change your surroundings: add color and brightness and scent to bring those "winter blues" under control.

Boudica

Notes:

February 26
Monday

 2nd ♋

Color of the day: Ivory
Incense of the day: Peony

Daylight Ritual

By this time of the winter you may be experiencing "winter blues" from dreary days, too much snow, or being cooped up in your house too long. Chase the blues away by making the house springlike. Get "daylight" bulbs and replace your

February 27
Tuesday

 2nd ♋

Color of the day: Black
Incense of the day: Sandalwood

Fire Ritual

Winter is a perfect time to work fire magic and deepen your connection with the element of fire. In Celtic communities, the domestic fire was located in the center of the

room. In the days before electricity, the warmth, light, and many blessings of fire were central to survival and daily life. Fire could also be used magically to bless and protect. New babies were handed back and forth over the flame three times, or carried three times around the fire sunwise by the eldest person in the family or community. Give thanks to the spirit of fire for its gifts and powers. Familiarize yourself with the colors, energies, patterns, and essence of the flame. Sacred objects may be purified and consecrated by passing them over or quickly through a flame.

Sharynne NicMhacha

Notes:

February 28
Wednesday

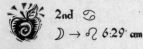 2nd ♋

☽ → ♌ 6:29 am

Color of the day: Topaz
Incense of the day: Maple

Open Chakras Spell

When discussing the chakras, we generally think about the seven main ones, but there are also two pairs of chakras at the soles of the feet and centers of the palms. These chakras are our connections to the world, influencing how we feel and sense the world around us. Opening them will allow you to connect to the elements, which is great when you need to be grounded or balanced. To open them, sit with your legs crossed and your bare feet sticking outward. Place your hands, palms up, on your lap. Place quartz crystals on each palm and by each foot. Chant the following:

> Feet and hands,
> Wheels of light,
> Open now,
> Shining bright.

Repeat for a few minutes. When the chakras are open, you might feel a normal warmness or tingling where they're located. Now take a few moments to feel each element and engage each sense. Enjoy the sensation.

Olivia O'Meir

Notes:

March is the third month of the Gregorian calendar, and it was the first month of the Roman calendar. The month is named for the Roman god of agriculture and war, Mars. Its astrological sign is Pisces, the fish (February 18–March 20), a mutable water sign ruled by Neptune. March is a month of transition between winter and spring. Daffodils begin to brighten the early garden. The sap rises, and robins return. In the hardware stores, shelves are stocked with garden tools and packages of flower and vegetable seeds. Still, late-season snowstorms are not unusual in March. Ostara, the main holiday of the month, celebrates the lengthening hours of daylight and the awakening of the Goddess. Eggs, whether dyed or intricately decorated, are popular seasonal symbols of life and fertility. St. Patrick's Day, March 17, is rich with Pagan symbolism. For example, the shamrock was once used to depict the three aspects of the Goddess. Sunny, breezy days encourage kite-flying, another seasonal activity. Kites are magical because they soar toward the realm of spirit. The ancients used the March wind to carry their wishes to the divine. The winds of March bring the promise of a new season and a fresh start. March's Full Moon was called the Storm Moon, and it remains a potent time to work magic for change and renewal.

March 1
Thursday

2nd ♌

Color of the day: Purple
Incense of the day: Cedar

Protection Ritual

A folk rhyme tells us that March roars into our lives like a lion. Stormy weather can create havoc and damage in our lives. To protect your property and loved ones from the damage of storms, exercise good common sense and take care of the physical aspects of protection. Secure your property and plan for disaster in the material realms. Then magically cast a circle around your living space and property. Call in spirits and totems of protection, making sure to use symbols and beings that are important and sacred to you. Call these in at each of the cardinal directions of north, east, south, and west, and then call in center.

> Spirits of power, spirits
> of each direction,
> I call on you for strength
> and protection.
> Save us from danger and
> guard our peace,
> Our vigor, security, and
> safety increase.
> So mote it be!

Take up your circle and live in safety. If you move or leave the place, release these powers, thanking them for their service to you.

Gail Wood

Notes:

Holiday lore: On March 1, Roman matrons held a festival known as Matronalia in honor of Juno Lucina, an aspect of the goddess Juno associated with light and childbirth. Some records indicated that her name was derived from a grove on the Esquiline Hill where a temple was dedicated to her in 375 BC. Whenever a baby entered the world in Roman times, it was believed that the infant was "brought to light." Women who worshipped Juno Lucina untied knots and unbraided their hair to release any entanglements that might block safe delivery.

 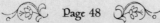

March 2
Friday

 2nd ♌
☽ → ♍ 4:32 pm

Color of the day: White
Incense of the day: Jasmine

harmony Water

> 3 tbs. basil
> 1 tbs. rosemary
> 1 tbs. mint

Cover the herbs with six cups of hot water and consecrate them. Steep the herbs for thirteen minutes and then strain the liquid. The water can be added to floor wash, used on counters and in corners, or bottled and sprinkled on altars or in rooms where arguments have occurred.

Cerridwen Iris Shea
Notes:

March 3
Saturday

 2nd ♍
Full Moon 6:17 pm

Color of the day: Blue
Incense of the day: Ginger

Goddess Spell of Three

Today is an especially enchanting day, capturing the magic of the number three as the third day of the third month. Combine this with the energies of the Full Moon in a lunar eclipse and you have a particularly potent day for magic. Protection magic has been practiced for thousands of years to help us manage conflict and ward off negative energies such as malicious gossip. Talk is cheap, or so they say. But when that talk is about you and portrays you in a not-so-positive light, it not only hurts—it can be damaging! Keep in mind that most bad gossip and rumors are fueled by emotions of jealousy or fear, or both. For a spell to protect against malice, you will need a small bowl of salted water, a small bottle with a stopper, a stick of frankincense (small enough to fit in the bottle), and a white candle. Visualize yourself surrounded in a circle of blue light. Light the incense and imagine the smoke as the nasty words you have heard. Place the incense stick into the bottle and seal it in. The lack of oxygen will extinguish the stick. Use wax from the white candle to seal the bottle stopper. Bury the bottle and imagine the intensity of gossip dissipating.

Emely Flak

Notes:

March 4
Sunday

Purim

 3rd ♏

Color of the day: Gold
Incense of the day: Juniper

Overspending Spell

There are a few magical activities you can use to help banish overspending. Use a penny bank or a savings account as a way to watch overspending and create prosperity. Buy a small notebook and bless it. Consider it a magic mirror, able to reflect the truth. You want the book to show you the reality of your spending habits. After blessing it, use it to keep track of the next few weeks' purchases. At the end, review them. Where is your money going? Having this self-knowledge can help you cut

back on unnecessary items. You can also use an affirmation when out at the mall or the market, such as,

> A penny saved is a penny earned

or

> I only buy what I need, not just what I see

or

> I don't need this right now. My money only goes where I allow.

Olivia O'Meir

Notes:

March 5
Monday

 3rd ♏
☽ → ♎ 4:25 am

Color of the day: Lavender
Incense of the day: Parsley

End of Hibernation Spell

Watch for the emergence of hibernating animals. Since the most ancient times, the appearance of these mysterious creatures was considered to be a positive and

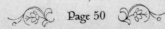

important omen that heralded the return of spring. Spiritually, they symbolize energies associated with deep trance-sleep, reawakening, and rebirth. What animals first appear in the area where you live? Bears and other mammals, reptiles, insects, and serpents all have their gifts and spiritual wisdom. Create a darkened atmosphere in which to drum, rattle, or chant to connect with the energies and life-wisdom of these sacred beings. Spend some time in complete darkness to see what energies exist in this place. Remember that the primal darkness is a place of transformation, and that what seems to be "empty darkness" actually contains the whole of creation and of existence. See how you are different after emerging from an extended ritual period in this sacred place.

Sharynne NicMhacha

Notes:

March 6
Tuesday

3rd ♎

Color of the day: White
Incense of the day: Lilac

household Protection Spell

Use some household spices today to banish negativity and create a protective energy throughout your home. Taking a jar of basil, a bowl of water, and some salt, sit in or near the center of your home. Invite the spirits of the directions, your own personal guardians, and the spirit guardian of this place to join you in this work. Offer the basil and salt to the sky, Earth, and center, asking that the guardians present might increase their protective energies. Sprinkle a small amount of each in the water. Take the water to the front door and pour it onto the ground as an offering to the guardian spirits of the place. Then take the basil and sprinkle a small amount in each room of your house, imagining the protective energy filling the space. Be sure to place some beneath all the beds, windows, and doors.

Kristin Madden

Notes:

 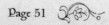

March 7
Wednesday

 3rd ♎

☽ → ♏ 5:16 pm

Color of the day: Yellow
Incense of the day: Poplar

Good Fortune and Cheer Spell

This spell is not only fun to do, but has a way of increasing your own good fortune and cheer. Let's face it—a little extra good karma won't hurt any of us. To work this spell, take a handful of spare change and charge it with happy vibrations and blessings of good luck. Say, "For any and all who may find this gift, it is my will that they feel their spirits lift. Blessings of luck and good fortune I send, only positive things will this spell rend." Repeat the verse nine times. Throw the change onto a sidewalk, parking lot, or anywhere people are apt to find it. Smile and say, "Make it so, make it so!" Keep note of the good things that come to you today.

                                   Tammy Sullivan
Notes:

Holiday lore: Although the month of June is named for Juno, principal goddess of the Roman pantheon, major festivals dedicated to her are scattered throughout the year. For instance, today marks Junoalia, a festival in honor of Juno celebrated in solemnity by matrons. Two images of Juno made of cypress were borne in a procession of twenty-seven girls dressed in long robes, singing a hymn to the goddess composed by the poet Livius. Along the way, the procession would dance in the great field of Rome before proceeding ahead to the temple of Juno.

March 8
Thursday

 3rd ♏

Color of the day: Crimson
Incense of the day: Pine

Stone Spell for Financial Stability

Most of us have some financial responsibilities that have become burdensome, causing us worry and stress. We must learn to forgive ourselves and know that these problems are not the end of the world. To help with this process, wrap a dollar bill around a stone. As you visualize the stone absorbing your financial worries, leaving

the money free and unhindered, say these words:

> Stone of earth, relieve
> my stress,
> My future plans will all
> be blessed.
> Of money woes let me
> be free,
> For good of all, so mote
> it be.

Bury the stone in the ground and keep this dollar on your altar or in a safe place where you'll never spend it.

Ember

Notes:

Holiday lore: While most holidays across the world celebrate the lives and achievement of men, March 8 is one day wholly dedicated to the achievement and work of women. Originally inspired by a pair of mid-nineteenth-century ladies' garment workers' strikes, today the holiday is little known in its country of origin; though this day's legacy is clear in March's designation by the U.S. Congress as Women's History Month. Throughout the month, women's groups in American towns hold celebrations and events, concerts, exhibitions, and rituals that recall heroic and gifted women of every stripe.

March 9
Friday

 3rd ♏

Color of the day: Purple
Incense of the day: Sandalwood

Melting Ice Love Spell

It's springtime, and love is in the air. It's time to rekindle the passion in yourself as you get ready for the dating scene. Place ice cubes in a clear pitcher or vase. Light a rose-colored candle anointed with rose

oil and place it behind the container so the light reflects on the ice cubes. As the cubes melt, watch the cubes reflect the light and color and think about the perfect love in your life. Don't use images—use emotions. How does it feel to be in love? How do you want to feel? How should you feel? Feel the love in you as the ice melts away. Remember those feelings and look for those feelings to be reflected back to you by the people you meet. Chances are, if you feel those emotions from another, it could lead to a romantic encounter!

Boudica

Notes:

teacher in the Neoplatonic school. She also served as a librarian in the famous Library of Alexandria. Alas, some Christian priests did not approve of a Pagan scholar, especially a woman who taught men. They incited riots against her and eventually orchestrated her murder by a mob. She is a martyr among scholars, women, and Pagans alike. Honor her memory on Hypatia's Day by doing things that promote learning and tolerance. Donate money or books to your local library in her name. Teach a workshop on math magic. Attend a lecture at a local university or bookstore. Study Pagan history. Learn about gender studies. Put your energy where your ethics are. You don't have to work a spell to work magic—you can work magic by choosing actions that help shape the world in a more positive direction.

Elizabeth Barrette

Notes:

March 10
Saturday

 3rd ♏

☽ → ♐ 5:37 am

Color of the day: Black
Incense of the day: Rose

Silent Magic Spell

Hypatia of Alexandria was a scholar, a mathematician, and a

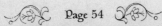

March 11
Sunday

Daylight Saving Time begins 2 am

 3rd ♐
4th quarter 11:54 pm

Color of the day: Orange
Incense of the day: Juniper

Tea Spell

Banish those minor yet annoying health problems with this simple spell. While some of the claims are in dispute, it is still widely agreed upon that tea holds many health benefits. For this spell, you will need a box of your favorite tea. Remove the plastic wrappings from the tea box and place it in a window where the moonlight can fall upon it. You want to visualize the moonlight infusing the tea with her calming energy. The next day when you fix yourself a cup of tea, feel its healthy energies working their way throughout your body, fortifying it against weakness.

Laurel Reufner

Notes:

March 12
Monday

 4th ♐
☽ → ♑ 4:34 pm

Color of the day: Silver
Incense of the day: Sandalwood

Transition Meditation

March is a month of transition. Sometimes it can truly be difficult to adjust to those changes, and a simple grounding and centering meditation may be just the thing you need to empower yourself while going through changes in your life. Find a comfortable place to lie down. Close your eyes and breathe slowly and deeply. Picture the Earth slowly turning on its axis while circling the Sun. Know that you are part of that movement. Think about the fact that there is movement with purpose all around you. Realize that change is movement. There is a purpose, and a season for all things, including you. Relax and go with the flow.

Paniteowl

Notes:

March 13
Tuesday

4th ♑

Color of the day: Scarlet
Incense of the day: Chrysanthemum

Wash Away Winter Spell

Now the streams begin to flow again and ice begins to melt on rocky ledges. This ritual serves as a symbolic way to wash away winter's grip. Fill a spray bottle with bottled spring water and add about three tablespoons of rose water. Spray on at least one window on each side of your house, inside and out. Then wipe with a clean cloth. Also spray any glass panes in your front and back doors. If you have any rose-water solution left, spray and wipe mirrors throughout your home also. Pour any leftover water mixture outdoors, around your home or in your garden, to encourage the awakening Earth.

James Kambos

Notes:

March 14
Wednesday

4th ♑
☽ → ♒ 10:52 pm

Color of the day: Brown
Incense of the day: Juniper

Positive Mercury Energy Spell

Wednesday is ruled by the planet Mercury, which is concerned with matters of business, travel, and communication. All can go awry when Mercury goes "retrograde." Due to orbital mechanics, the planet seems to move backwards for a while, as seen from Earth. During this time, Mercury's energy is warped or unavailable. So here's a spell to store up positive Mercury energy for use as a shield during retrograde periods. You will need a silver coin (use a "Mercury dime" if you can get one) and a blue candle. Place the coin on your altar and light the candle. Then say:

> Mercury, god of all swift things,
> Lend our tongues grace and our thoughts wings.
> Let business soar and travel fly,
> When you dance back—ward in the sky.

Focusing on the coin, pour energy into it, emphasizing ease of motion and communication. When finished, blow out the candle. Carry the coin while Mercury is retrograde.

Elizabeth Barrette

Notes:

The black candle flames to remove negativity.

The energies combine as one, through space and time.
Bring to me success and wealth with a spell that rhymes.

Ellen Dugan

.Notes

March 15
Thursday

 4th ≈

Color of the day: White
Incense of the day: Neroli

Banish Your Money Worries

Spring is just around the corner. This is a great time of year to banish financial difficulties and worries over money. The timing is perfect. You have a Jupiter day for prosperity and a waning Moon phase to banish financial worries. Burn a green pine-scented candle to encourage prosperity, and burn a black patchouli-scented candle to remove the worry and stress you may have over money. Repeat the following charm three times. When finished, allow the candles to burn in a safe place until they go out on their own.

I burn this green candle
to promote prosperity,

Holiday lore: Why is March 15 so notorious? On this date in 226 BC, an earthquake brought the Colossus of Rhodes—one of the Seven Wonders of the Ancient World—to its knees. But a more famous event likely accounts for the notoriety of the "Ides of March." Julius Caesar's rule, somewhere along the way, became tyrannical. In February of 44 BC, Caesar had himself named Dictator Perpetuus—Dictator for Life. Brutus assassinated him on March 15. Caesar's murder was foretold by soothsayers and even by his wife, Calpurnia, who had a nightmare in which Caesar was being butchered like an animal. Caesar chose to ignore these portents and the rest, of course, is history.

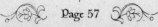

March 16
Friday

 4th ≈

Color of the day: Coral
Incense of the day: Carnation

Cleansing Ritual

Spring is a good time to cleanse yourself of any excesses. This can include an excess of anything, like energy, drink, emotion, or exercise. A ritual bath can help us renew. First set the mood, using a few candles to light the room. Music can also set the tone; use classical to relax or pop ballads for romance. Fill the tub with warm to hot water and add two or three drops of cleansing oil to the bath. Try rosemary, juniper, and lavender. Step into the bath and relax. See all the impurities drain out of you. Sit for about ten to fifteen minutes. When you get out, drain the tub. At this point, you can dry off or take a quick cool shower to rinse off.

Olivia O'Meir

Notes:

March 17
Saturday
St. Patrick's Day

 4th ≈
D → H 1:30 am

Color of the day: Brown
Incense of the day: Dill

Keys to Saint Patrick

The only evidence that Saint Patrick ever existed is based on his supposed autobiography discovered some five hundred years after it was written. Most likely Saint Pat is really a Christianized version of the shamrock god, *Trefuilngid Tre-eochair*, "Triple Bearer of the Triple Key." The god is described in *The Yellow Book of Lecan* as a giant man, thirty feet high, with waist-length golden hair. He carried a sacred branch— the triple key on which grew hazelnuts, apples, and acorns—and is said to have brought the art of storytelling to the Irish. As you celebrate Saint Patrick's Day, use the energies of these three fruits in your magical workings today. Hazelnuts bring wisdom and luck, apples bring romance, and acorns bring prosperity.

Lily Gardner

Notes:

Holiday lore: Much folklore surrounds St. Patrick's Day. Though originally a Catholic holy day, St. Patrick's Day has evolved into more of a secular holiday today. One traditional icon of the day is the shamrock. This stems from an Irish tale that tells how Patrick used the three-leafed shamrock to explain the Trinity of Christian dogma. His followers adopted the custom of wearing a shamrock on his feast day; though why we wear green on this day is less clear. St. Patrick's Day came to America in 1737, the date of the first public celebration of the holiday in Boston.

March 18
Sunday

 4th ♓
New Moon 10:42 pm

Color of the day: Yellow
Incense of the day: Pine

New Moon Beginning Spell
Tonight marks the New Moon, also known as Dark Moon. At this time, the Sun and Moon are in conjunction. The Moon rises and sets at the same time as the Sun. The feminine, reflective lunar energy merges with the masculine, expressive solar energy. The New Moon is an auspicious time to start new projects. Spring is also a time of fresh beginnings, rebirth, and burgeoning growth. For this spell, you will need two packets of seeds: white moonflowers and red morning glories. You will also need a white candle. Play some lunar- and solar-themed music in the background, too. Light the candle, and tuck the edges of the seed packets under the candleholder. Imagine the plants sprouting and say:

> Moon and Sun and Earth
> and Space,
> Lend me power
> in this place.
> Space and Earth and
> Sun and Moon,
> Let these flowers
> flourish soon.

Now visualize the vines twining together as they grow, bedecked with the red flowers of the Sun by day and the white flowers of the Moon by night. Use this image to balance the solar and lunar energies within yourself. Let the candle burn out, and plant the seeds in your garden.

Elizabeth Barrette

Notes:

 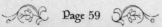

March 19
Monday

1st ♓
☽ → ♈ 1:41 am

Color of the day: Ivory
Incense of the day: Sage

Saint Joseph's Spell

Every Witch should have the Saint Joseph spell for selling a home. I've used it twice with great success and have passed it on to friends who were amazed by the results. One word of advice: your asking price must be fair and reasonable in order for the spell to work. You'll need a statue of Saint Joseph, a green candle, and pine oil. Cast your circle and dress the candle with pine oil and light it. Say:

> To sell this house is my plan,
> A buyer comes with money in hand.
> All love and light, the sale is done.
> And I shall prosper, the battle won.

Visualize a "sold" sign in your front yard and a moving van filled with your furniture parked on the street. Everyone is happy. Bury the Saint Joseph statue upside down, facing your home. Leave him buried to bless the new owners.

Lily Gardner

Notes:

March 20
Tuesday

Ostara – Spring Equinox –
International Astrology Day

1st ♈
☉ → ♈ 8:07 pm

Color of the day: Red
Incense of the day: Myrrh

Ostara Egg Spell

The Spring or Vernal Equinox marks the pagan holiday of Ostara. It is a time of balance and a celebration of the return of springtime. The spring holidays of many cultures celebrate with symbols of birth, growth, and fertility, such as rabbits and eggs. Most cultures gave their goddesses springtime gifts of eggs to ensure fertility and blessings. The yellow of the yolk symbolizes the returning Sun and the white shell represents the purity of the returning Maiden Goddess. Across time and across cultures, people decorated eggs in colors and symbols to reflect newness and freshness. The beautifully and intricately decorated Ukrainian eggs are made by writing eggs with beeswax in a *batik* or resist method. The dye is applied and the waxed part remains uncolored. Called *pysanky*, the Ukrainian word for decorated egg, they are prized works of art. Witches can do a magical pysanky by writing or drawing glyphs, runes, and symbols on the eggs and then dyeing them. Focus your intention on writing and decorating a hardboiled egg; use meaningful symbols and then dye it an appropriate color. Focus your wish or desire into the egg. Offer thanks to the Goddess, then eat it mindfully, imagining the new magic filling you like the pure sunlight of the season.

Gail Wood

Notes:

March 21
Wednesday

 1st ♈

☽ → ♉ 1:15 am

Color of the day: White
Incense of the day: Honeysuckle

Notice Me Spell

Having trouble getting your efforts noticed at work? We all seem a little invisible sometimes, but it's frustrating when it seems to last forever. Gather a small mirror, green and red candles, and some coffee beans. Light the candles, with the red to the left of you and the green to the right. Sit looking into the mirror and tell yourself some of the reasons you are not getting noticed at work and then the reasons you deserve to be more noticed. Let the candle burn down, then place the mirror on a windowsill for three nights. Place the coffee beans upon the mirror to absorb the negative "I'm invisible" energy. Dispose of the beans and keep the mirror somewhere at work.

Laurel Reufner

Notes:

March 22
Thursday

 1st ♉

Color of the day: Green
Incense of the day: Sandalwood

Improved Finances Spell

Tax time will soon be upon us. It is the perfect time to work a little magic to ensure our financial obligations are met without too many challenges. Take a cloth pouch and place it on your altar. Light a green candle and cedar incense. Inside the pouch place cedar chips (money), chamomile flowers (money), basil (money and protection), two magnets (attraction), coins, a pinch of salt, bloodstone (money), a dollar bill, and a horseshoe drawn on green paper. Close the pouch. Raise your left hand, palm up, and place your right hand on the bag. Pull energy from the universe with your left hand and push it into the bag with your right. Affirm:

> I pull to me Financial prosperity. I will meet all of my obligations with no trouble. With harm to none, my will is done!

Tammy Sullivan

Notes:

Holiday lore: Cybele was the Great Mother of the gods in Ida, and she was taken to Rome from Phrygia in 204 BC. She was also considered the Great Mother of all Asia Minor. Her festivals were known as *ludi*, or "games," and were solemnized with various mysterious rites. Along with Hecate and Demeter of Eleusis, Cybele was one of the leading deities of Rome when mystery cults were at their prime. Hila'aria, or "Hilaria," originally seemed to have been a name given to any day or season of rejoicing that was either private or public. Such days were devoted to general rejoicing and people were not allowed to show signs of grief or sorrow. The Hilaria actually falls on March 25 and is the last day of a festival of Cybele that commences today. However, the Hilaria was not mentioned in the Roman calendar or in Ovid's *Fasti*.

March 23
Friday

 1st ♉

☽ → ♊ 2:06 am

Color of the day: Rose
Incense of the day: Evergreen

Chili and Chocolate Spell

Venus in Taurus relishes the good things in life. Today is the perfect day to stir up a little passion and recognize that you deserve the very best! So pick up a fabulously rich chocolate brownie mix and some mild red chili powder. Make the brownies according to the manufacturer's directions but add about a teaspoon of red chili powder to the mix. Bake as directed and let them cool a bit before indulging your body and mind on the exceptionally sensual warmth of these little treats. With each bite, allow your senses to fully experience the tastes and textures. As these fill you with good feelings, say to yourself:

> I am a sensual,
> loving being. I deserve to
> give and receive pleasure
> and love. I give thanks
> for/call to me the friends
> and lovers that share in
> the passion and honor of
> my spirit.

Kristin Madden

Notes:

March 24
Saturday

1st ♊

Color of the day: Gray
Incense of the day: Almond

Seed-Sowing Spell

In Scotland, grain seeds were ritually prepared before being sown in the sacred Earth. Three days before sowing, the seeds were sprinkled with clear, cold water as the water-bearer walked in a sunwise direction. The person performing the ritual invoked the Christian Trinity in later times, a replacement for the Sacred Three (the gods, the ancestors, and the land) which were venerated in earlier times. This ritual took place sometime between Imbolc and Spring Equinox. A variety of charms were spoken before the seeds were planted:

I will sow the seed,
I will face the wind
And throw a gracious
handful on high.

The dew will come to
welcome every seed
That lay in sleep since
the coming of cold.

They will inhale life from
the soft wind,
And every seed will take
root in the Earth.

Sharynne NicMhacha

Notes:

March 25
Sunday

1st ♊
☽ → ♋ 5:49 am
2nd quarter 2:16 pm

Color of the day: Amber
Incense of the day: Lavender

Closing Ritual

Throughout our lives, we face situations where a chapter closes. It can be a relationship that has ended, an accident, or leaving a job. In many cases, we continue to think about it in a way that consumes too much of our precious energy. When this happens, we need to acknowledge closure. Missing from our modern society are formal rituals or ceremonies for closure, to affirm an ending. With every ending comes a new beginning. If there is something in your life that requires a close to make way for new opportunities and energies to enter your life, try this spell. Select an item that represents the old chapter that you will discard or destroy. For example, this can be a business card from your previous employer or a photo of your ex-lover. Wrap it in an envelope with these written words:

Times of old now set
free, make way a new
start for me.

Emely Flak

Notes:

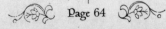

March 26
Monday

2nd ♋

Color of the day: White
Incense of the day: Basil

Joseph Campbell's Birthday

The mythologist Joseph Campbell used many myths and legends to illustrate the potential that each of us has, and encouraged people to "follow your bliss." As we sit with our family in the evenings, we can read to our kids or grandkids these same stories, these myths and legends that are the foundations of our beliefs and practices today. There are also modern "myths" that we can read to our kids. Look for stories that spark the mind and take the imagination beyond the limits of traditional education. Encourage your children and grandchildren to dream, and to follow their bliss. Healthy young minds need this "dream stuff" so they may never know limitations on their imaginations. An unlimited imagination has endless possibilities.

                                    Boudica

Notes:

March 27
Tuesday

2nd ♋

☽ → ♌ 1:04 pm

Color of the day: Maroon
Incense of the day: Daffodil

Controlling Change Spell

Changes in our lives can be unsettling, and we often wish we had more control over those situations. Here is a simple spell casting that helps do just that. Using a cotton swab dipped in lemon juice, write a brief description of the things that bother you the most on a piece of parchment paper. It could be that you are not seeing all the possibilities in the changes you fear. Now heat an iron and press it to the parchment. You will see the writing come clear. As you do this, say the following:

> These are changes I can
> see, make their nature
> clear to me!

You will be able to find solutions to the problems caused by change once you see the whole picture.

                                    Paniteowl

Notes:

March 28
Wednesday

2nd ♌

Color of the day: Topaz
Incense of the day: Musk

Home Guardian Spell

The wisest in the craft employ a guardian at the front entry to ensure only positive vibrations come into the home. One of the best living guardians is a cactus plant. Any one of the desert family will do, and the spikier the better. To activate a cactus as your new guardian you must feed it. Guardian food is simple: just smash together eggshells, coffee grounds, and a tiny splash of beer. As you bury the food in the plant's pot say:

> I charge you with the protection of my home and all within it.
>
> I trust that you belong to me and I belong to you. We will tend to each other.
>
> Be blessed in the light, Be blessed through the night.
>
> We shall be friends. It is so!

Tammy Sullivan

Notes:

March 29
Thursday

2nd ♌
☽ → ♍ 11:27 pm

Color of the day: Turquoise
Incense of the day: Sandalwood

Prosperity Charm

This Thursday, close to the Spring Equinox, is a wonderful time to set financial goals for the coming year. Make a list of these goals. Charge one shiny new penny (preferably the current year) with each goal (one penny per goal). Place the pennies in a green bag with springs of rosemary and vetivert and one whole nutmeg. Keep the bag in a safe place. Each time you achieve a goal, cross it off your list, remove a penny from the bag, thank and bless it, and then leave it in a place where someone else will find it, so the luck passes forward.

Cerridwen Iris Shea

Notes:

ing herbs to draw a lover to you, and to ensure your lover will always think about you.

James Kambos

Notes:

March 30
Friday

 2nd ♏

Color of the day: Pink
Incense of the day: Carnation

Flower Love Magic

Daffodils, hyacinths, tulips, and many other spring-blooming flowers are announcing the arrival of spring in my garden. Many of these flowers have been used by magicians for centuries to enhance love and fertility spells. Blooming crocus attracts love; a pot of crocus grown indoors increases loving vibrations. During love spells, place a bouquet of daffodils on the altar; a vase of daffodils in the bedroom also increases fertility. Use the dried flowers of hyacinth in love sachets to draw love to you. Tulips, with their rounded cup shape, have a feminine quality and can be placed on the altar during a love spell. And both pansies and violets used in bouquets increase lust and draw love. Plant pansies with other love-attract-

March 31
Saturday

2nd ♏

Color of the day: Blue
Incense of the day: Thyme

Luna Ritual

Today is the festival of Luna, the Roman goddess of the Moon. Gather together some fresh white flowers—roses, carnations, or lilies—and arrange them in a water-filled vase. Arrange a few moonstones on your work surface and light white and silver candles. Take a moment to honor one of the oldest mother aspects of the goddess of the Moon. Luna is a powerful deity; she is especially fond of magic users and will gently make her presence known in your life, no matter what the Moon phase.

On this night I honor Luna, goddess of the Moon.

In this enchanted time, listen to this Witch's tune.

Grant me illumination and grace, Lady I pray,

May I be respectful of your magic every day.

Ellen Dugan

Notes:

April is the fourth month of the year of the Gregorian calendar and the first month of the astrological calendar. Its astrological sign is Aries, the ram (March 20–April 20), a cardinal fire sign ruled by Mars. The name of the month comes from the Latin *aprilis*, which derives from *aper*, or "boar," as April was thought to be the month of the boar. April delights the senses: the damp earth after an April rain and the sweet fragrance of flowering crab apple trees. Some of the most dramatic changes in nature occur in April. Buds swell and growth begins. Flowering trees such as dogwood, redbud, cherry, and apple are at the height of their beauty. Azaleas burst into bloom, bringing color to shady places. And, weather permitting, gardens and fields are tilled, ready to receive early crops of lettuce, spinach, and onion. Birds add to the beauty of April—not only are they busy building nests, but their songs now greet us on misty spring mornings. Holidays of the month are April Fools' Day, when we celebrate the Trickster, and Earth Day on the 22nd, which makes us aware of environmental issues. The beautiful flowering trees of the month gave April's Full Moon its charming old-fashioned name—the Pink Moon. Early herbalists and folk magicians used this period to enhance spells concerning health and general well-being.

April 1
Sunday

April Fools' Day – Palm Sunday

 2nd ♏
)) → ♎ 11:43 am

Color of the day: Yellow
Incense of the day: Jasmine

Fool's Laughter

Laughter is good for body, mind, and spirit, and April Fools' Day is all about having some good-natured fun while we remember to not take ourselves too seriously. Today, create the magic of joy as you fully experience the playfulness of this very silly holiday. Start first thing in the morning. Get up and go to the mirror. Smile on purpose until you really feel the silliness of what you are doing. Make faces at yourself in the mirror until you laugh. Then decide on something silly and fun to do today. Jump in mud puddles, have a pillow fight—whatever makes you smile. Throughout the day, tell silly jokes, poke a little fun at yourself, or play good-natured jokes and help those around you to laugh. And when you retire for the night, fill your mind with the fun and laughter of the day.

Kristin Madden

Notes:

April 2
Monday

2nd ♎
Full Moon 1:15 pm

Color of the day: White
Incense of the day: Coriander

Night Blooming Bouquet Spell

As you go about your esbat celebrations, don't forget to bring the blessings of the Full Moon inside your home. Fill a white or crystal vase with fresh water and add a moonstone and a quartz crystal. Finish filling the vase with primrose blossoms, jasmine flowers, four o' clocks, and nicotiana blooms. Fern fronds, hosta leaves, and Queen Anne's lace add the perfect finishing touch. Before you take the vase inside, enchant it by the light of the Moon. Say:

> Beauty by night
> To please my sight;
> Divine, fragrant blooms
> To scent my rooms.
>
> I ask the Lady's bless-
> ings she will bestow
> To wherever this vase
> may go.

Chant the verse at least nine times. Place the flowers anywhere you desire, knowing that blessings will follow. Once the blooms are spent, save the petals for potpourri. To renew the scent, add fresh flowers. You may use this potpourri as a base for any type of blessing spell. Additional flowers, crystals, or herbs can be blended in according to intent. This potpourri can be simmered or simply placed in an open container. As long as the petals remain, the Lady's blessings and the Full Moon's power will flow through your home.

Tammy Sullivan

Notes:

April 3
Tuesday
Passover begins

3rd ♎

Color of the day: Red
Incense of the day: Jasmine

Divination Tool Blessing Spell

Spread out patterned cloth of purple, white, and green, and on it place a white candle for clarity and purity of purpose and a purple candle for enhancing mental acuity

and psychic powers. Mix together nutmeg with sage to promote psychic ability and clear, pure thought, and place a small dish of the herbs on the cloth. In the center, place your divination tools. Include any deities and symbols important to you, or that you want to connect to your divination work. Begin by humming a long single tone while envisioning a clear white light around the cloth. Light the candles, calling in the spirits that you wish to witness this blessing. Pick up your divination tool and hold it to your heart. Cast your awareness to your feet, and envision the energy of the Earth coming up through your feet, through your body to your heart. Envision this Earth energy now mingled with yours, coming out through your heart and into your tool. Feel this energy surround your hands and the tool and quietly allow the energy to permeate them. Place the tool in the herbs and cover it while visualizing clarity, purity of purpose, and psychic knowledge and wisdom. Next, pass the tool over the purple candle and envision the tool opening and communicating deep wisdom. Then pass the tool over the white candle while envisioning purity and clarity. Hold the tools to your heart again, breathing deeply, to create a vital connection with you. When you are finished, extinguish the candles. Wrap the tool in the cloth, place it on top of the dish of herbs, and leave it on your altar for three days. After that, unwrap it and use the tool with honor, wisdom, and deep knowledge.

Gail Wood

Notes:

Come home safe
From harm and strife,
For we will build
A better life.

Put a picture of your loved one in your locket, and your picture in the locket of your loved one.

Paniteowl

Notes:

April 4
Wednesday

3rd ♎
☽ → ♏ 12:35 am

Color of the day: Brown
Incense of the day: Gardenia

Protection of Loved Ones Spell

Many of us have loved ones who are far away, and we worry about their safety, so a sympathetic charm is appropriate to wear yourself or send to your loved one. Take a lock of your hair, a sprig of rosemary, a sprig of lavender, and a gold ribbon. Weave the three items in a small braid and place them in a locket. As you weave, say this chant:

Over and under,
Around I do bind.
I am yours,
And you are mine.

April 5
Thursday

3rd ♏

Color of the day: Green
Incense of the day: Eucalyptus

Lady Luck Charm

In ancient Rome, today was dedicated to Fortuna, goddess of good fortune and happiness. On this day, also known as Lady Luck Day, Fortuna gave success and prosperity to those with pure and positive intentions. On her special day, make a charm that harnesses the magic of the oak tree. You will need three acorns, three oak leaves, and a piece of green or gold cloth. Tie the oak leaves and acorns in the fabric and keep them in your purse to attract wealth and fortune. As you make the charm, say these words and maintain a positive image in your mind about fortune:

> Lady Luck,
> Goddess of Fortune,
> All my gifts I appreciate
> And thank thee.
> There is room in my life
> For additional abundance
> If that is to be!

Emely Flak

Notes:

were deep seated, and when we read through the accounts of his teachings, we see that he lived by his word. Take time on this day to reflect on other teachings of love and peace by teachers who walk in the world today. There are many modern-day teachers of this message, such as the Dalai Lama. Look at how love and peace can be part of the spiritual path you follow. How can you achieve peace and love in your own life?

Boudica

Notes:

April 6
Friday

Good Friday – Orthodox Good Friday

3rd ♏
☽ → ♐ 12:56 pm

Color of the day: Rose
Incense of the day: Jasmine

Teacher Magic

On this day a teacher is honored for his beliefs and his teachings. His beliefs in peace and love

April 7
Saturday

3rd ♐

Color of the day: Gray
Incense of the day: Ylang-ylang

Banish Those Creative Blocks Spell

Banish those creative blocks. Go get some paper and pencils or crayons. Light any color of candle that your whimsy chooses. You will need a fireproof dish and something

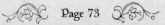

to set it on as well. Sit down by the candlelight and cover the paper randomly with words if you're a writer or hastily drawn images if you're an artist. Do not censor yourself, but just let it all flow onto the paper. There. You have just created probably the ugliest thing you will ever create. Now burn it.

Laurel Reufner

Notes:

April 8
Sunday
Easter – Orthodox Easter

 3rd ↗
$\mathcal{D} \rightarrow \text{♑} $ 11:36 pm

Color of the day: Gold
Incense of the day: Jasmine

Renewal Spell

As the Christian world celebrates renewal, use this time to meditate on the shared beliefs of cultures and religions of the world. Resurrection stories have been found in nearly every culture throughout history. (This is also the day the Japanese celebrate Buddha's birth-

day.) Obtain some seeds for a plant you'd like to grow. Prepare the soil—or container—and plant the seeds. Visualize the life cycle of growth, death, and rebirth that occurs in the natural world as you plant these seeds. Think of all the patterns of renewal that occur in life and keep this in mind as you tend your young seedlings. As you plant them, chant the following:

Cycles of life,
waxing, waning,

Success and strife,
waxing, waning,

Tides of power,
waxing, waning,

Seed to flower,
waxing, waning.

Ember

Notes:

April 9
Monday

 3rd ♑

Color of the day: Lavender
Incense of the day: Clove

Sticky Situations Spell

This is a spell that calls on the energy of the Moon's day and the lunar tides of the waning Moon. This is a glamour type of color magic that will help you to blend in and go unnoticed in sticky situations. Wear lunar-associated colors such as silver, white, and the palest blues. Before you head out for the day, enchant your outfit so you can go about your business quietly, without a fuss. This spell helps to smooth out obstacles that are in your way, and to calm tempers. Once you are dressed and ready to go, look at yourself in the mirror and cast the spell.

> The lunar shades of magic are white, silver, and blue,
>
> Concealment and illusion they'll grant softly to you.
>
> Now smooth all obstacles that are in my way,
>
> Peace and quiet are the order of the day.

Ellen Dugan

Notes:

April 10
Tuesday
Passover ends

 3rd ♑
4th quarter 2:04 pm

Color of the day: White
Incense of the day: Jasmine

Making Sunshine Spell

Tuesday is Mars' day. Mars is not just the god of war—he also oversees agriculture and forward motion. Today, take a few minutes to stand out in the sunlight. Feel the positive, forward-moving energy flow from the Sun into your body. Allow yourself to fill with energy. Now go out into the world and perform an anonymous act of kindness for a stranger. Tonight, prepare a feast of fiery foods in honor of Mars. Bless and consecrate the food to him and offer up your random act of kindness in his honor. Don't rush through the

meal—eat mindfully, enjoying all of it. Feel Mars' strength, confidence, and ability to handle all situations fill you through food, word, and deed.

Cerridwen Iris Shea

Notes:

Light the candle and start writing about the problem. Let your thoughts come streaming out and write down everything, pleasant and not. Start with one word and keep writing, even if you have to write the same word over and over. You'll notice one concept that seems to catch your attention. This will often be the core of the problem. After you find that, you can focus on finding a solution.

Olivia O'Meir

Notes:

April 11
Wednesday

 4th ♑
♑ → ♒ 7:23 am

Color of the day: Topaz
Incense of the day: Ginger

Core of the Problem Ritual

Occasionally, a problem is so confusing that we don't know how to start searching for an answer. Sit in front of a yellow or white candle with a parchment and pen. Say:

> For this problem
> In my mind,
> A solution I have
> Yet to find.
>
> Clarity seems hard won,
> But I will search
> Until I'm done.
>
> So mote it be.

April 12
Thursday

 4th ♒

Color of the day: Turquoise
Incense of the day: Cedar

Reaping Money Spell

Thursday belongs in the jurisdiction of Jupiter. The Roman god Jupiter dealt with matters of law and stability. This is a good day for spells about money, prosperity, and business. Many magical traditions recognize the "Rule of Three," that whatever you do comes back to you

three times over. Here is a prosperity spell using the energy of Jupiter and the Rule of Three. For this spell, you will need three dollar bills (or use larger bills, if you can afford to) and some green thread. Roll each bill into a tight tube, always rolling toward yourself. Tie each tube with green thread. Then put the money into a charity box, and say (silently if someone is watching):

> I reap what I sow.
> I get what I throw.
>
> Money come, money go.
> Money come!

Your generosity will draw prosperity to you.

Elizabeth Barrette

Notes:

istorical note: On April 12, 1961, Yuri Gagarin piloted the first manned spaceship to leave the pull of our planet's gravity. This achievement is given much less attention than it deserves; part of it is politics, since Gagarin was a cosmonaut for the Soviet Union. Part of it, too, is time; today, space pilots live and work for months aboard space stations, so a simple space flight seems routine. Still, Yuri Gagarin's 108-minute flight in space represented a triumph of science and engineering, and also broke a psychological barrier. It was literally a flight into the unknown. "Am I happy to be setting off on a cosmic flight?" said Yuri Gagarin in an interview before the start. "Of course. In all ages and epochs people have experienced the greatest happiness in embarking upon new voyages of discovery . . . I say 'until we meet again' to you, dear friends, as we always say to each other when setting off on a long journey."

April 13
Friday

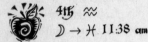

4th ≈
☽ → ⊬ 11:38 am

Color of the day: Pink
Incense of the day: Cedar

April Showers Healing Spell

The rains of April are healing and cleansing. You can use the April rain to help heal a broken heart. You'll need a small dish or saucer from a flowerpot, some potting soil, and a rainy day. Pack the soil firmly into the dish. With your finger trace the form of a heart into the soil and draw a line through the heart. Place the dish on the ground during a rain (select a place where it won't be disturbed). After the rain, the heart shape should have disappeared. End the ritual by crumbling the soil onto the ground as you say:

> With earth and rain,
> I have healed my pain.

James Kambos

Notes:

April 14
Saturday

4th ⊬

Color of the day: Blue
Incense of the day: Nutmeg

Kwan Yin Travel Spell

April fourteenth isn't the best day to travel, but if it's not your wish to stay home today, use this travel spell. Take a map that includes both your starting point and your destination. Hold a piece of malachite in your passive hand and chant this mantra to Kwan Yin, goddess of compassion and protection. Beloved as a mother figure, Kwan Yin pays special attention to travelers. Say:

> Om Mani Padme Hum

which means "Hail to the Jewel in the Lotus." Continue to chant this prayer until you feel the light of Kwan Yin's blessing, then trace your route with a piece of malachite. Visualize yourself traveling safely and smoothly. Carry the malachite on your person throughout your journey.

Lily Gardner

Notes:

April 15
Sunday

 4th ♓
☽ → ♈ 12:46 pm

Color of the day: Amber
Incense of the day: Patchouli

Tax Day Spell

April fifteenth, or tax day, comes as a great worry and relief to many Americans. However, sometimes our worries persist even after the tax returns have been filed. Once you send out your return, take a big breath in and out. In a fire-safe container, light charcoal and burn some sandalwood, patchouli, or any rich-smelling herb. Take a spare copy of your tax return (make sure you have another copy or two for your files) and write on it:

> Goddess and God, bless
> my tax return. May it
> be accurate and cor-
> rect. May I receive the
> most money. May it get
> to the Internal Revenue
> Service safely. So mote
> it be!

Take the papers, light them on fire, and place them on the herbs. Burning the sheet will allow your prayers to be heard on the wind.

Olivia O'Meir

Notes:

April 16
Monday

 4th ♈

Color of the day: Ivory
Incense of the day: Poplar

I Am So Relieved Meditation

In the United States, federal income taxes are due on April 15. The day after is usually a time of considerable relief because the nerve-wracking, tedious work is finally finished—or an extension has been filed! Now is the time to get rid of the tension stored in our bodies and relax. Put on some music you can move to—something with a strong beat. Jump up and down while envisioning the tension, anxiety, and stress streaming off your body and into the earth. Do that for at least two to three minutes. Turn off the music and come to stillness, either sitting or standing. Breathe deeply and fully three times. Breathe again and envision the calm blue light of

relief filling you from the top of your head to the tips of your fingers and the tips of your toes. Breathe in this light for two to three minutes. When you are done, touch your hand to the floor and send thanks to Mother Earth.

Gail Wood

Notes:

potato in a place where it will not be disturbed. As you bury the potato, say the following:

> As the New Moon rises,
> all things will renew. I
> charge this battery with
> new resolve! My plans
> will now come true!

Picture the energy of the potato battery recharging your own energies and giving new excitement to your project.

Paniteowl

Notes:

April 17
Tuesday

4th ♈

New Moon 7:36 am

☽ → ♉ 12:11 pm

Color of the day: Scarlet
Incense of the day: Peony

New Moon Charging Spell

Gather together a potato and two pennies. Cut the potato in half and carve a circle in the middle of each half large enough to hold a penny. Around the pennies carve the name of the project to which you'd like to give energy. Put the potato pieces back together, and on the night of the New Moon bury the

April 18
Wednesday

1st ♉

Color of the day: White
Incense of the day: Pine

Creativity Spell

The grain goddess Ceres is celebrated this week. As the mother of all living things, we pray to Ceres for creativity. In fact, *Ceres* and *create* share the same root word. The most potent way to invoke this goddess of grain is to make hot cereal or bake bread. Using the fertile energies of wheat, raisins, and hazelnuts, make a loaf of bread today. As you prepare the dough, invoke Ceres to help you lead a more creative life.

1 cup white flour
1 cup whole wheat flour
1 tsp. cinnamon
1 tsp. allspice
1 beaten egg
1/2 cup applesauce
3 tbsp. oil
1/2 cup maple syrup
1 cup raisins
1 cup finely chopped
    hazelnuts

Mix all ingredients together. Bake in a 350° oven for forty-five to fifty minutes or until a toothpick inserted in the middle of the loaf comes clean.

Lily Gardner

Notes:

April 19
Thursday

 1st ♉
𝄯 → ♊ 11:51 am

Color of the day: Purple
Incense of the day: Maple

Bread Blessing
Today is the last day of the feast of the Roman goddess Ceres and the anniversary of the official dedication of her temple. On this day, honor Ceres, goddess of grains and cultivation, with the following ritual to increase abundance in your life. Bake a loaf of bread or buy a loaf from a bakery and serve it at a meal. Use this blessing before eating:

> We are grateful for the hands that created this food, and to the elements of earth, air, fire, and water for making life possible.
>
> Ceres of the flowing grain, abundance to our table bring.
>
> Blessed be.

Ember

Notes:

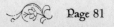

April 20
Friday

 1st ♊

☉ → ♉ 7:07 am

Color of the day: Coral
Incense of the day: Sage

Confidence Spell

Sometimes the most positive magical act we can do is to work for self-love and to boost our confidence. So during this waxing Moon phase, work to increase your self-love, confidence, and positive outlook with this spell. You will need one pink rose-scented candle, a coordinating holder, a few rose-quartz stones for self-love and to promote happiness, a pleasing photo of yourself, and a safe flat surface to set up the spell. Arrange the components of the spell as you like, then repeat the charm three times:

> Friday is devoted to the goddess of love,
>
> Lady, hear my call for help, answer from above.
>
> Bless me with confidence, joy, and contentment true,
>
> May my actions be loving in all that I do.

For the good of all, with harm to none,

As I will so mote it be, an let it harm none.

Ellen Dugan

Notes:

April 21
Saturday

 1st ♊

☽ → ♋ 1:50 pm

Color of the day: Indigo
Incense of the day: Ginger

Margarita Magic

Margaritas have all the ingredients you need to add a little magic to any gathering. Salt on the rim of a glass is protective. Lime juice, both purifying and protective, is often used in love spells. Other flavors bring in energies you desire. For luck and fortune, add orange juice. Strawberry will intensify your love-and-luck margarita. A dash of mint will add healing and prosperity.

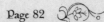

Start with a pitcher, filled halfway with ice cubes. Pour enough lime juice over the ice to fill the pitcher half full. Add your favorite magical flavors until the pitcher is three-quarters full. Then top it off with equal parts tequila and brandy or sparkling water. If your guests are magically inclined, have everyone take a moment to imagine all the blessings they want filling the glass before drinking. Be sure to toast to your blessings and enjoy!

Kristin Madden

Notes:

mary or lavender essential oil. Place the picture under the candleholder. Light the candle and place your hands on the table on either side of it. Take a calming, centering breath and visualize the person well and healthy again. Pour your energy into the image and send it spiraling out in his or her direction, asking that the energy be accepted if it is the best for the ill person. Ground yourself and cut the link to the spell. Allow the candle to burn out, or burn it over several days.

Laurel Reufner

Notes:

April 22
Sunday
Earth Day

 1st ♋

Color of the day: Orange
Incense of the day: Lilac

healing Energy Spell

Send healing energy to a loved one quickly and easily with this simple spell. You will need a picture or other representation of your recipient, a green candle, and rose-

April 23
Monday

 1st ♋

☽ → ♌ 7:38 pm

Color of the day: Silver
Incense of the day: Cinnamon

Children's Day Spell

Do you remember the fun times in your childhood when there were no limitations to your dreams? In Turkey, today is Children's Day, acknowledging their country's most

 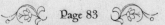

precious resource. If you can, spend some time with a child today, or watch children playing in a nearby park. Observe their boundless energy and unadulterated view of the world. Watch how they enjoy simple things like watching a butterfly or playing on a swing. In adulthood, it's easy to overlook the pleasure that simple things can bring. At the end of the day, reflect on the things you enjoyed as a child and ask yourself if you can occasionally indulge in the same activities. As you are contemplating, and perhaps listening to music you enjoyed in your younger years, say to yourself:

> A child I was
> And can sometimes be.
>
> I will release the
> Inner child in me.

Emely Flak

Notes:

April 24
Tuesday

 1st ♌
2nd quarter 2:35 am

Color of the day: Black
Incense of the day: Lavender

Warding Spell

Spring cleaning also means it is time to ward your home against all the outside nasties that may try to find their way into your home. Start with the windows and doors, drawing chalk banishing pentagrams on them and saying:

> Goddess shield,
> Goddess surround,
> house and hearth,
> home and ground.

Clean your house with a traditional smudging and wash entryway floors and windows with protective ingredients such as water, apple-cider vinegar, and mint. Mint added to your smudge also adds to the protection. Black stones, such as black tourmaline or onyx, placed by the door will deflect negativity and guard against dangers entering your home.

Boudica

Notes:

April 25
Wednesday

 2nd ♌

Color of the day: Yellow
Incense of the day: Juniper

honoring Kore

Spring is in the air. Tulips and daffodils are blooming. Now is the season of Kore, the Child-Goddess. She is the daughter of Demeter, Goddess of Grain. Kore gives the flowers their rainbow of colors. In autumn, she descends to the underworld to spend winter with her husband Hades; there she rules as queen of the dead. But in spring, Kore returns to the world above and to her mother. Rejoicing at her return, the Earth bursts forth with blossoms. Many rituals at this time of year honor Kore. You may wish to greet her with a bouquet of spring flowers and an invocation such as this:

> Tulips in the meadow,
> Crocus on the hill.
> Spring is slow in coming,
> But we know it will.
>
> Kore paints the flowers
> Yellow, pink, and white.
> Join us, Child-Goddess,
> Bring the waxing light!

Elizabeth Barrette

Notes:

April 26
Thursday

2nd ♌
☽ → ♍ 5:24 am

Color of the day: Crimson
Incense of the day: Pine

Simple Money Spell

Some of the most effective magic is also the easiest to perform. To work this spell, take a green candle and anoint it with blessed oil. Roll it in a mixture of ground cinnamon, cloves, ginger, and nutmeg. Surround the candle with a circle of salt. Say:

> I call to the earth, the air,
> the flame, and the sea.
> To this spell add
> strength and energy.
>
> Where I have needs,
> so shall they be met.
> No more worry,
> no need to fret.

I am in need of (insert amount needed here).

I call this unto myself!
With harm to none,
I will that this be so!

Light the candle and allow it to burn itself out. Carry a chip of the wax with you.

Tammy Sullivan

Notes:

on the Goddess as Protector of the Beasts, asking her blessings on your animals and the animals of others.

hoof and claw,
fur and paw.
fin and feather,
Love together.

Ask for her blessings on this companionship, and for long life, protection, and good health for your companion. Give your animal to her care, and honor her once a year in thanks for your animal's continued life and health.

Gail Wood

Notes:

April 27
Friday

2nd ♏
Color of the day: Purple
Incense of the day: Jasmine

Animal Protection Spell
Pets and animal companions come to us in all sizes, shapes, and species. We celebrate our love and relationship with them. Spend a little time with your animal companion, taking and communing. Sing, croon, and express your love to them. Think too of all the other people who have animal companions and love them. Breathe deeply and call

April 28
Saturday

2nd ♏
☽ → ♎ 5:44 pm

Color of the day: Black
Incense of the day: Rose

Violet Love Spell
In many areas, an abundance of violets (both purple and white) appears to announce the coming of

May and its ancient festivities. These flowers have a most magical quality and appearance, and can be used in a variety of ways. Violets are edible, and in Scottish folk tradition violets were boiled in whey and given as a cool and refreshing drink to those suffering from fevers. Herbal practitioners used violets to treat many conditions, including "love-idleness." Women in ancient Scotland used a preparation of violets infused in goat's milk as a beauty cream, and violet petals soaked in white wine was a popular festive drink. Use sprigs of violets to decorate the home, create candied violets as a springtime treat, or float violets in your May Day punch bowl.

Sharynne NicMhacha

Notes:

April 29
Sunday

2nd ♎

Color of the day: Yellow
Incense of the day: Juniper

Garden Magic

The hoe is a simple garden tool, almost unchanged in appearance since ancient times. Our early ancestors' hoe was a long stick with the shoulder blade of an animal attached to it. Ask any gardener what a hoe is used for, and they'll tell you it's for turning the soil and preparing a seed bed—but they fail to mention the "magic" found in a hoe. When you use a hoe in the spring, you are connecting with Mother Earth after winter's rest. You can feel it: the sun on your face, the feel of the hoe in your hand, and the scent of the moist, fresh earth. But the most magical part of all is when you lean on your hoe after a session in the garden. That is when you learn the secret only a fellow gardener would know: the Earth belongs to us, and we belong to the Earth.

James Kambos

Notes:

April 30
Monday

 2nd ♎

Color of the day: White
Incense of the day: Sandalwood

Floralia Spell

Today is a precursor to May Day. It is the Roman festival honoring the goddess Flora, thanking her for keeping the flowers and grains blooming. Traditionally, people created flower wreaths and attended the theater. Give thanks to Flora by tending your houseplants today. Feed them, trim them, and let them know how much they matter. Build a floral wreath to hang on your door. If you don't want to go to a show, create one with your family and friends in honor of Flora.

Cerridwen Iris Shea

Notes:

May is the fifth month of the year. Its astrological sign is Taurus, the bull (April 20–May 21), a fixed earth sign ruled by Venus. The month is named for Ma'a, a Roman goddess and mother of the god Hermes. May is known as the queen of months. It is a month of lushness and beauty. The main holiday is May Day, or Beltane. This sabbat celebrates the sacred union of the Goddess and God. It is a celebration of growth and fertility. A traditional part of this holiday is the Maypole, usually a fir tree with the side branches removed—a symbol of fertility. Since growth is a theme of May, another central figure of the month is the Green Man, a male form covered with leaves and branches. He is an ancient nature spirit who brings life to the fields and forests after the long winter. Flowers are popular during Beltane rites, which gives May's Full Moon its lovely name—the Flower Moon. Many flowers and trees that bloom this month are associated with magic. Lilacs were originally grown near the home to repel evil. Wild blue violets can be used in love magic. A steaming infusion made with dried dandelion root was used to contact spirits. The hawthorn tree is also associated with May folk magic. To make a wish come true, burn three hawthorn branches in a Beltane fire.

May 1
Tuesday
May Day – Beltane

2nd ♎

☽ → ♏ 6:41 am

Color of the day: Scarlet
Incense of the day: Coriander

A Maypole Spell for Beltane

Beltane celebrates the union of the Goddess and God. The Maypole, which is an important part of Beltane rites, also serves to symbolize the bonding of the feminine and masculine elements. All trees are connected with the Goddess and God. Their roots are nourished by Mother Earth, and their leaves absorb the life-giving rays of Father Sun. But the Maypole has even deeper magical associations with the divine couple. Traditionally, most Maypoles are made from fir trees stripped of all but their highest branches. The fir tree, being evergreen, symbolizes everlasting life, and the trunk is a male fertility symbol. The act of erecting the Maypole is rich with symbolism. When the Maypole is placed into the ground, we are witnessing the divine marriage of the Goddess and God. Since most of us can't erect a Maypole, try this ritual instead. Select a wooden dowel three feet high. Think of what you wish to achieve this spring and summer. As you do this, anoint the dowel with olive oil infused with sweet woodruff or pine. Insert the dowel into a flower pot filled with garden soil and sprinkle the soil with salt water. Wrap your Maypole with white and red ribbons—white represents the mystery of death, red is the color of life. Wrap a garland of flowers around the pole and think of your desires coming to fruition. Around the base of the Maypole, place strips of paper upon which you've written your wishes. Keep these until they manifest in your life. At Beltane, the Earth is alive and magic is afoot.

James Kambos

Notes:

May 2
Wednesday

 2nd ♏

Full Moon 6:09 am

Color of the day: Brown
Incense of the day: Honeysuckle

Full Moon Faery Spell

Since this Full Moon is so close to the sabbat of Beltane, its energies will transfer over to our Full Moon celebration as well. Tonight would be a wonderful night to call on the faeries. Ask them to watch over your gardens and to protect your outdoor magic space. Perhaps you can leave a small cake or cookie, or even a few quartz points tucked in the plants and flowers, as an offering to the garden faeries. Begin the spell as the Full Moon rises. Once it is visible from your garden, repeat the following:

> A Full Moon the night
> after Beltane adds
> blessings galore,
>
> I ask the Fae to protect
> these gardens that
> I adore.
>
> Weave your magic with
> mine, circle around this
> place,
>
> As we bless and protect
> our sacred garden space.

> Ellen Dugan

Notes:

May 3
Thursday

 3rd ♏

☽ → ♐ 6:47 pm

Color of the day: Green
Incense of the day: Neroli

Prosperity Talisman

The recent Full Moon lends power to this talisman, energizing it to draw prosperity. Find a special coin such as a Sacagawea dollar, half-dollar coin, or a foreign coin—something unusual that you can easily identify and won't spend. Carry it with you every day in your purse or pocket so you'll never be without money. The point is to have a special monetary item to keep with you at all times. Hold the coin between your palms and visualize your purse or wallet filled with money. Charge the coin:

May I always have funds
to serve my needs:

I ask this out of love,
not greed.

                                    Ember
Notes:

seeds will give you a definite boost
of energy. There is no specific spell
to use as you plant your seeds: your
own intent is already invested in the
planting.

                                    Paniteowl
Notes:

May 4
Friday

3rd ♐

Color of the day: White
Incense of the day: Vanilla

Connecting With the Earth Spell

The Sun stays longer every
day, and it's time to put down
roots. Planting a seed helps you get
in touch with Earth energies whether
you have a garden or a windowsill
in an apartment. Choose seeds that
will help you connect with things
that are important to you. If you are
a Kitchen Witch, you can start an
herb garden. If you feel that you are
a healer, plant some medicinal herbs
that will help you focus on your healing. If you are a person in need of
grounding and centering, then flower

May 5
Saturday
Cinco de Mayo

3rd ♐

Color of the day: Gray
Incense of the day: Dill

Anti-Meddling Spell

A mother nearly always acts
in the best interest of her
child—or at least she believes she
does. Sometimes, the mother of
our beloved partner acts in a way
that astounds us. This behavior has
become the source of many "mother-
in-law" jokes. If you have a meddle-
some mother-in-law, try this spell.
This aims to reduce her influence,
but with positive intent. You have
probably heard about attracting more

flies with honey than vinegar. This doesn't mean you need to be sickly sweet with your challenging family member. Be assertive without being aggressive. Place a photo of this person in a jar of honey and keep it in a place where she will never find it. As you close the lid, say these words:

> Your words, your actions,
> Too much they interfere.
> Even if they are well
> meaning,
> They no longer belong
> here.

Each time you see your mother-in-law, remember the photo and influence trapped in honey.

Emely Flak

Notes:

Holiday lore: Don't confuse Cinco de Mayo with Mexican Independence Day on September 16. Cinco de Mayo marks the victory of the brave Mexican army over the French at the Battle of Puebla. Although the Mexican army was eventually defeated, the *Batalla de Puebla* became a symbol of Mexican unity and patriotism. With this victory, Mexico demonstrated to the world that Mexico and all of Latin America were willing to defend themselves against any foreign or imperialist intervention.

May 6
Sunday

3rd ♐
☽ → ♑ 5:21 am

Color of the day: Orange
Incense of the day: Pine

Lemon Light Spell

With spring at its peak there is no worse time to be sick. Yet it is this time of year when many people suffer from horrible allergies and "summer colds." Lemons hold amazing healing properties. They purify and detox the body while stimulating energy and cheer. Build one lemon a day into your diet by adding a slice to each drink you consume. While slicing the lemon, visualize the juice as a golden light. See the light spreading warmth and healing throughout your body. If there are any dark spots in the body, the light quickly cleanses them and energizes them to a bright gold. Each time you take a drink, allow yourself a moment to visualize the light. The flavor of lemon is a good complement to water, tea, and seafood, among other edibles.

Tammy Sullivan

Notes:

May 7
Monday

 3rd ♑

Color of the day: Lavender
Incense of the day: Basil

Merry Meet Spell

People often feel awkward when meeting new people, fearing that they will create a bad impres-

sion. But when you are comfortable with a situation, you will put others at ease and the meetings will indeed become merry. To become more comfortable with meeting new people, stand in front of a mirror. Shrug your shoulders, squirm, tug at your clothes, and do all of those awkward, fidgety motions you do when you are nervous and uncomfortable. Take three long, deep, cleansing breaths, and renew your connection with Mother Earth. Now look in the mirror and smile. Cheerfully say, "Bright blessings. Greetings and merry meet." Watch the person respond with smiles and handshakes. Keep on practicing until you feel comfortable with what you look like when greeting new people. Take a deep breath and go forward to comfortably greet new people, using words and greetings appropriate to the situation. Merry meet, merry part, and merry meet again.

Gail Wood

Notes:

 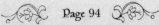

May 8
Tuesday

3rd ♑
☽ → ≈ 1:48 pm

Color of the day: Red
Incense of the day: Chrysanthemum

Ginger Ale Energy Drink

When you have a moment when you will not be disturbed, hold a can of ginger ale in both hands and close your eyes. Visualize the creative energies and the "heat" of the ginger filling this drink completely. Imagine that the can tingles with all the beneficial energies bubbling about inside. If there is something specific you need energy for today, imagine that situation flowing well and ending with great success. Then drink the ginger ale as you normally would. With each sip, feel the energy filling your body and mind as the water permeates your cells. Feel each carbonated bubble bringing energy to your awareness and releasing it into you to use as you need.

Kristin Madden

Notes:

May 9
Wednesday

3rd ≈

Color of the day: Yellow
Incense of the day: Evergreen

Spirit Banishing Spell

During the Feast of Lemures ("restless dead") the ancient Romans exorcised malevolent ghosts of the dead from their homes. The ghosts were appeased by offerings of beans and salt-wheat cakes prepared by the Vestals. We can clear our homes of unwanted spirits by placing offerings of cakes and drink on our table at dinner for them. After the meal, place the offerings outside to draw the spirits out of your home. Draw banishing symbols in chalk and hang mirrors on the doors, windows, or anywhere a spirit could re-enter your home. To keep the spirits away from your door, hang sprigs or a small wreath of marjoram, mint, and rosemary.

Boudica

Notes:

May 10
Thursday

3rd ≈≈
4th quarter 12:27 am
☽ → ♓ 7:31 pm

Color of the day: Purple
Incense of the day: Eucalyptus

Night Vision Spell

The sun sinks past the western horizon. The stars come out. But no Moon rises to light the way, so the night stays dark. Velvet shadows cloak the world. If only you could see like a cat! Here is a spell to improve night vision. You'll need a tiger's eye stone, preferably in an earring, but a pendant or ring will do. You'll also need incense associated with vision, such as frankincense or clove, or a psychic vision blend. Light the incense and wave the stone through the smoke, saying:

> Tiger's-eye stone
> that I hold,
> Flickering with
> brown and gold,
> Lend me vision
> beyond sight
> As cats see through
> dark of night.

Wear the tiger's eye at night, and it will help you see in the dark.

Elizabeth Barrette

Notes:

May 11
Friday

 4th ♓

Color of the day: Pink
Incense of the day: Sandalwood

Venus Love Spell

Friday belongs to Venus, who oversees matters of love and relationships. Her metal is copper; her colors are green and pink. Call on the power of Venus to bring fresh romance into your life. For this spell, you will need a copper bracelet made of two wires twisted together; and a stick of incense congruent with Venus, such as cherry or ylang-ylang. Decorate the altar with sensual flowers like gardenias and orchids. Light the incense. Wave the bracelet through the smoke, saying:

> As wires twine,
> May our hearts do:
>
> Two become one,
> And yet still two.

 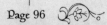

Venus, bring love
And make it true.

Meditate on how the two strands of the bracelet support each other without losing their own identity. Wear the bracelet when you go out looking for romance, and it will help attract partner compatible to you.

Elizabeth Barrette

Notes:

you are trying to break. Be specific in your goals and put them on the branch. Now, with great intent, break the branch into pieces as small as you can manage. Toss the pieces back on the ground and walk away.

Laurel Reufner

Notes:

May 12
Saturday

4th ♓
☽ → ♈ 10:19 pm

Color of the day: Brown
Incense of the day: Thyme

Bad habit Spell

Use this month's New Moon to help finally break a bad habit you've been wrestling with. Take a walk outdoors where there are trees and the occasional fallen branch. Pick up one of those branches lying on the ground, take out a marker, and write on it the name of the habit

May 13
Sunday
Mother's Day

4th ♈

Color of the day: Yellow
Incense of the day: Coriander

honoring Our foremothers

Every Mother's Day, we take time to honor the women who gave birth to us. What about honoring our spiritual foremothers? Who has influenced you and your path? Was it an ancestor, a writer, a social leader, a Pagan priestess, or a goddess? Take a few moments and meditate. Next, list the names on a paper and add a description of what they mean to you. Write from the heart. Pour your emotion into the paper. Later that night, create a simple ritual to honor those women. During the ritual, light a white candle for remembrance. Burn some sacred incense, like sandalwood or Nag Champa. In the ritual, read what you wrote aloud. As you read it, let love and admiration fill you. Give thanks for the contributions these women made to your path.

Olivia O'Meir

Notes:

May 14
Monday

 4th ♈
☽ → ♉ 10:48 pm

Color of the day: Silver
Incense of the day: Coriander

Seed Blessing Ritual
Today is the feast day of "Cold Sophie," the last of the Ice Saints. The "Ice Saints" (Mamertus,

Pancras, Gervais, and Cold Sophie) celebrate their feast days from May 11 to 14, a time that is traditionally frosty. Use this day to prepare your garden for planting and to bless your seeds and bedding plants. Spread your seed packets on your altar or kitchen table. Burn a green candle dressed with vetivert. Spend some time visualizing the beautiful garden you'll have this year. Say:

> Blessed Gaia, mother of
> us all,
> Make these plants grow
> strong and tall.
>
> A bountiful harvest,
> Flowers sweet and
> bright,
> Blessed by the Sun and
> pale moonlight.

Wait until the New Moon of May 16 before planting.

Lily Gardner

Notes:

May 15
Tuesday

4th ♌ ♂

Color of the day: White
Incense of the day: Myrrh

I Guess We're Not in Kansas Anymore Meditation

L. Frank Baum, the creator of Oz and the *Wizard of Oz* books, was born on this day in 1856. He reminds us that ordinary "Kansas" is only in our mind and that wonder is found everywhere. To find wonder in your life, settle yourself in your meditative space. Light some sandalwood incense and breathe deeply. See your life as it is with all its dissatisfactions and distractions. Breathe into that and quickly out of it to move outside yourself. Ask the spirits you hold dear to show you the magic and wonder of your life. Breathe deeply, listening to and watching this powerful moment of stillness and darkness. Wonder is everywhere in your life. Notice that and open to it. When you are finished, come back to your space. Record your newfound wisdom by writing, drawing, or other means. Most of all, live your life as one full of magic and wonder.

Gail Wood

Notes:

May 16
Wednesday

4th ♌ ♂
New Moon 3:27 pm
☽ → ♊ 10:34 pm

Color of the day: Topaz
Incense of the day: Sage

Self Love Spell

Our capacity to love others goes only as deep as our capacity to love ourselves. Begin by making four separate lists of what you like about yourself, one for each element. Try to make these lists as complete as possible. Under the "earth" heading, list what you like about your physical body—not only how your body looks but how it feels and what it does. Under the "air" heading, list what you like about your mind. Include areas of knowledge in which you are expert and your mental talents. Under the "fire" heading, list your achievements and creativity.

 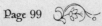

Under the "water" heading, list what you like about your relationships and social skills. Transfer your lists to pieces of rice paper. Now fill your bathtub and add some rose water. Add half a cup of sea salt to your bath. Now dip your "earth" list into your bath. The ink and most of the paper will dissolve in the bath. Light a stick of rose or lavender incense, and then dip your "air" list into the bath. Light a pink candle and dip your "fire" list into the bath. Dip your "water" list into the bath. Soak in the tub for at least twenty minutes. Feel yourself soaking up the attributes you love about yourself.

Lily Gardner

Notes:

always seems to come like a fresh breath of air. Focus this energy in a completely spontaneous ritual. Just go outside to a safe and comfortable place. Come as you are to the circle. Lift your hand and cast the circle, feeling the energy moving through you. Call the elements in whatever way you choose and sense them flowing through you. Just let the words come out; don't worry about being eloquent. Feel how free ritual and life can be. After the ritual, think about how you can bring this freedom into other parts of your life. Start small: a quick change to your day could make a difference, like going out for a walk during your lunch hour or treating yourself to a guilty pleasure.

Olivia O'Meir

Notes:

May 17
Thursday

 1st ♊

Color of the day: Turquoise
Incense of the day: Cedar

Banishing Rigidity Spell

Banishing the winter's stiffness and rigidity can help us enjoy the warm spring weather. The spring

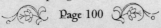

May 18
Friday

 1st ♊

☽ → ♋ 11:38 pm

Color of the day: Coral
Incense of the day: Cedar

home Guardian Spell

The wisest in the craft employ a guardian at the front entry to ensure only positive vibrations come into the home. One of the best living guardians is a cactus plant. Any one of the desert family will do, and the spikier the better. To activate a cactus as your new guardian you must feed it. Guardian food is simple: just smash together eggshells, coffee grounds, and a tiny splash of beer. As you bury the food in the plant's pot say,

> I charge you with the
> protection of my home
> and all within it.
> I trust that you
> belong to me and I
> belong to you.
> We will tend
> to each other.
> Be blessed in the light,
> Be blessed through
> the night.
> We shall be friends.
> It is so!

> Tammy Sullivan

Notes:

May 19
Saturday

 1st ♋

Color of the day: Blue
Incense of the day: Ylang-ylang

Lilac Magic

The beautiful May-blooming lilac is one of the loveliest tokens of spring. But they are much more than beautiful shrubs with showy, sweet-smelling flowers. Originally lilacs were planted to repel all evil. Planted near the entryway, lilacs were believed to send out protective vibrations. When the flowers are cut and brought into the home they cleanse any living space. And they'll also remove any unwanted spiritual presence. Blue and white varieties work well for this purpose. Since lilacs are ruled by Venus, they are also used in love spells. Try placing some pink lilacs on your altar while performing a love spell. The dried flowers make a powerful addition to any love sachet.

James Kambos

Notes:

Consider how the grace, beauty, and loyalty of the swan can enhance your life. Write a journal entry or a story or a poem, or paint a picture or create a dance celebrating the swan. Then apply what you've learned to your daily life.

Cerridwen Iris Shea

Notes:

May 20
Sunday

 1st ♋

Color of the day: Gold
Incense of the day: Jasmine

Swan's Grace Spell

Swans are one of the most beautiful and magical creatures on the planet. They mate for life. They herald healing and transformation. Take today to honor swans and the blessings swans bring to your life. Find a depiction of a swan. It can be a painting or a statue or even a stuffed toy swan. Light a white candle. Hold the representation of the swan in your hands. Breathe deeply. Ground and center. Feel the essence of the swan. Feel your body opening, healing, transforming with grace and beauty. Notice how you hold yourself differently, how you move differently.

May 21
Monday

 1st ♋
☽ → ♌ 3:56 am
☉ → ♊ 6:12 am

Color of the day: Ivory
Incense of the day: Parsley

Invoking the Dagda Ritual

In Celtic tradition, the summer half of the year (Beltane to Samhain) was the male half, and the winter part of the year (Samhain to Beltane) was the female half. This was reflected in the veneration of certain gods and goddesses as well as in folklore traditions. The Irish celebrated Beltane at *Uisneach*, the cosmological center of Ireland. This was the home of the Dagda, a powerful god of abundance, fertility, and druidical magic. He owned a cauldron of inexhaustible nourishment and a staff with the powers of life and death. Invoke the Dagda by holding a cauldron in your left hand and a rod or staff in the right, chanting his three names:

> Great Dagda
>
> Noble One of
> Great Knowledge
>
> Great Father of Many
> Horses

until you see him in your mind's eye.

Sharynne NicMhacha

Notes:

May 22
Tuesday

 1st ♌

Color of the day: Black
Incense of the day: Daffodil

School's Not Over Yet Spell

School is almost out, and many kids will lose focus early, especially on those last days when you can feel summer in the air. A pocket-sized "focus" bag helps draw them back down to Earth. Making one can be a project both you and your child work on together. Start with a base of salt and a quartz crystal, rosemary, and cedar shavings. Add to it items that remind the child of work still to be done, like a little doll-sized book or a paper with the date that school lets out written on it. The smell of the bag and its grounding contents will help your child remember to focus just a bit longer until school is out for the summer.

Boudica

Notes:

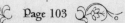

May 23
Wednesday

Shavuot

1st ♌
☽ → ♍ 12:26 pm
2nd quarter 5:02 pm

Color of the day: White
Incense of the day: Coriander

First Fruits Ritual

Shavuot, the "Feast of the Weeks," celebrates the Jewish harvest season. The term refers to the holiday's timing, seven weeks after Passover. Another name is *Yom Habikkurim*, the "Day of the First Fruits," when farmers brought their early harvest to Jerusalem in thanksgiving. After a long, dull winter, nothing compares to the taste of the first produce from garden and orchard. A few precocious varieties planted at Passover are ready by Shavuot—traditionally barley, but also greens like lettuce, fast-growing roots like radishes, and the earliest strawberries. Observing Shavuot encourages a plentiful growing season. Celebrate this holiday by setting aside some of your First Fruits, tied with a ribbon, for the gods and the animals. Hold a feast featuring the rest of your early crops, along with milk and honey, which are traditional foods available at this time of year. Decorate the table with tree branches and flowers.

Elizabeth Barrette

Notes:

May 24
Thursday

2nd ♍
Color of the day: Crimson
Incense of the day: Maple

Anti-Neglect Ritual

Go to a local plant nursery and look for plants being thrown away if they are past their prime and haven't been sold. Take a plant home and transplant it carefully. As you relieve the stress from the root ball, think about what you can do to relieve the stress of neglected children. As you tenderly nurture the plant, say these words:

> You are a child of the Earth, as am I.
>
> I see in you, all the children of the Earth, and I cry.
>
> With my hands I tend you, with my tears I water you, with my

 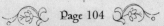

heart I love you, and
with my help may you
thrive.

Sympathetic magic works.

Paniteowl

Notes:

powerful!) Let the candle burn down
completely. It is done, except for
actually getting out of your home so
you have an opportunity to meet the
people the spell is drawing to you.

Laurel Reufner

Notes:

May 25
Friday

2nd ♏

Color of the day: Rose
Incense of the day: Carnation

New Friends Spell

Looking for new friends? Take
a piece of paper and, using
black ink, draw a series of concentric
circles upon it. As you draw, see
yourself in a setting you like with
your friends around you. The stron-
ger the visualization, the more you
can expect in the final results. Place
the drawing beneath a candle holder
containing a pink candle dressed with
rose geranium essential oil. (Use
the oil sparingly as the smell is very

May 26
Saturday

 2nd ♏
☽ → ♎ 12:16 am

Color of the day: Indigo
Incense of the day: Almond

Protection Glass Magic

For hundreds of years, glass
has been used in magic
and ritual. As this most functional
resource is now in every home, hotel,
apartment, and mode of transport,
you can perform magic with glass
at any time. It can be easily marked
with colorless liquid for protection.
To protect your home and your car,
prepare an oil blend of ten drops

frankincense oil to twenty milliliters of water. Dip your finger into this magical and protective blend and draw a pentagram on the inside of each window of your home (and car if you have one). As you draw each pentagram, say these words:

> May only love enter,
> May only love leave.
> My space is protected
> From all other unwanted
> energy.

Emely Flak

Notes:

May 27
Sunday

 2nd ♎

Color of the day: Amber
Incense of the day: Violet

Mars Energy Spell
During this waxing Moon, it's a great time to work spells for courage and passion. For this spell you will need a few holly leaves (a protective plant that aligns with Mars' fiery energies) and three small red candles in coordinating holders. Arrange the leaves on either side of the candles and take a moment to center and to contemplate your fears. Now face them. Take a deep breath and visualize the fears melting away, just as your spell candles will. Now light the red candles and repeat the spell three times:

> Mars' fiery energy will
> now flow about me,
>
> Passion, courage,
> and bravery, send
> swiftly to me!
>
> By all the magical
> powers of three
> times three,
>
> My worries no longer
> have power over me.

Allow the candles to burn in a safe place until they go out on their own.

Ellen Dugan

Notes:

May 28
Monday
Memorial Day (observed)

 2nd ♎

☽ → ♏ 1:11 pm

Color of the day: Lavender
Incense of the day: Rose

In Memoriam

In memory of those who have given their lives for the greater good, clear a table and cover it with a white tablecloth. Place a bouquet of flowers, perhaps forget-me-nots if you can find them, in the center of the table along with three candlesticks holding three white candles. As you light the first candle, say:

> I light a candle for all those who have fought for freedom
>
> hail the honored dead!

Light the second candle, saying:

> I light a candle for all those who have fought for tolerance and truth
>
> hail the honored dead!

Light the third candle, saying:

> I light a candle for all those who have fought to protect those who cannot protect themselves
>
> hail the honored dead!

Take a moment to be silent, honoring their memories and giving thanks for all they have done for this world, and for you personally.

Kristin Madden

Notes:

Holiday lore: Opinions are divided concerning the origins of the holiday of Memorial Day in the United States. This is a day set aside for honoring the graves of American war dead. While most historians credit the origins of the custom to Southern women, there is also a rumor, historically speaking, of an anonymous German who fought in the American Civil War (no one is sure on which side). At the end of the war, this soldier was allegedly overheard commenting that in the Old World people scattered flowers on the graves of dead soldiers. In May of 1868, a Union army general suggested to Commander John A. Logan that a day be set aside each year to decorate Union graves. Logan agreed, and he set aside May 30 for this ritual. His proclamation acknowledged those "who died in defense of their country" and "whose bodies now lie in almost every city, village, or hamlet churchyard in the land." This patriotic holiday was later amended to include all the dead from all the wars, and its date was shifted to a convenient Monday late in May.

My body this item
does adorn,
May it serve me well.

Keep me from harm
whenever it's worn,
May it serve me well.

Ember

Notes:

May 29
Tuesday

2nd ♏

Color of the day: Gray
Incense of the day: Rose

Jewelry Amulet Spell

It's easy to make any piece of jewelry you own into a protective talisman. Choose your favorite ring, necklace, earrings, bracelet, or other jewelry item that you wear often. First, clean the item with whatever method is safest for that type of jewelry. If in doubt, use water and toothpaste. As you clean, imagine any negative energy associated with the item being cleared away. Next, charge the item by either allowing it to sit beneath the sunlight for a day or the moonlight overnight, or simply visualize your specific need as you hold the item in your hand. Finish by chanting:

May 30
Wednesday

2nd ♏

Color of the day: Yellow
Incense of the day: Gardenia

Clover Success Visualization

While in the shower this morning, imagine that you are walking through a field filled with beautiful plants. You see lavender, lily of the valley, and mint. Pass under a pecan tree and rest in its shade, listening to the sounds of a brook nearby. Feel the soft green grass beneath you and notice that there are clovers among the grasses. Small pink flowers adorn some of the clover stems. Suddenly you see a four-leaf clover, glowing with green and gold energy. It is there just for you, bringing you luck and aiding in all your endeavors. Ask if you should pick this clover and bring it back with you or if it should remain where it is, allowing you psychic access to its energy when you have need. Do as it asks with respect and go about your day knowing that you carry this luck everywhere.

Kristin Madden

Notes:

May 31
Thursday

 2nd ♏
☽ → ♐ 1:06 am
Full Moon 9:04 pm

Color of the day: White
Incense of the day: Pine

Perfect Vacation Earth Spell
The Blue Full Moon is the perfect time to work magic that focuses on long-term goals. This spell can work to make your next vacation perfect. You will need:

A cardboard box with a lid
Strong tape
A postcard of the desired destination
Two magnets
Spare change
Lavender
Basil
Orange zest
Any other item that reminds you of your dream vacation

Place the items on your altar. Hold your palms a few inches above them and say:

I cast off all negativity that may hinder this spell. I bless these tools to call forth my will. May the Lord and Lady fill this working with energy and light.

Move the box to the center of your work surface. Say:

Of the Earth, steady and sure, I trust in you to hold this magic pure.

Hold the postcard and visualize yourself in that place, smiling and happy. Place it in the box. Affirm:

This is where I will take my vacation.

Place the magnets in the box. Say:

> From the Earth comes
> the power to draw this
> desire unto me.

Sprinkle the basil in the box. Affirm:

> Any negativity which
> could hinder the perfect
> vibrations of this
> vacation is removed by
> the power of the Earth.

Sprinkle the orange zest in the box and say:

> From the Earth to the
> light, hold my spirit
> bright. Bring forth
> laughter, joy, and cheer.

Sprinkle the lavender in the box. Affirm:

> This vacation will be
> filled with happiness and
> be stress free. By the
> power of the Earth.

Place the spare change in the box. Say:

> here this vacation
> begins.

Place the lid on the box and say:

> This magic is strong, it
> cannot go wrong. I call
> this vacation unto me, so
> mote it be!

Tape the box shut and bury it under your favorite flowers.

Tammy Sullivan

Notes:

June is the sixth month of the year. Its astrological sign is Gemini, the twins (May 21–June 21), a mutable air sign ruled by Mercury. It is named for Juno, the principal goddess of the Roman pantheon and wife of Jupiter. She is the patroness of marriage and the well-being of women. June is a month of plenty. Mother Earth is young and fresh. The air is sweet with the age-old scent of freshly cut hay. Honeysuckle covers old fences and fills June afternoons with its perfume. In the fields, corn and wheat reach for the Sun. In the garden, bees dance among the roses and larkspur. In June, the ancients prepared for the longest day of the year on the main holiday of the month, the Summer Solstice, or Midsummer. Wooden hoops were set ablaze, through which livestock and humans would pass as an act of purification. Herbs such as vervain and rue were cut on Midsummer and hung over doors and barn stalls to provide protection. The wild white daisies that bloom now along country lanes and in meadows were considered magic, for they represented the Sun. By mid-month the heat of summer begins, which gives June's Full Moon its name: the Strong Sun Moon. The beauty of summer's first Full Moon is rivaled only by another glowing token of June, the twinkling firefly.

June 1
Friday

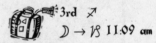

3rd ♐

Color of the day: Coral
Incense of the day: Geranium

Physical Protection Spell

In Japan, today is Clothes Changing Day, when uniforms and clothing officially change over to summer garb. At the same time, Japanese men and women pray for physical and bodily protection on this day. Hold a small stone in your hand while you visualize a sphere of white light surrounding you. Make sure that the bubble is clear and strong and goes all the way around you, above your head and beneath your feet. When the visualization is strong and firmly in place, clench the stone in your dominant hand and recite:

> Inside and out,
> head to toe,
> All harm,
> away from me go.
> Safety, go into this stone
> Shield, protect,
> and guard
> Skin, blood, and bone.

Carry the stone with you; grip it and visualize that protective light protecting you from injury.

Gail Wood

Notes:

June 2
Saturday

3rd ♐
☽ → ♑ 11:09 am

Color of the day: Blue
Incense of the day: Nutmeg

Goddess of the Angry E-mails

Now you've done it. An e-mail pissed you off. You were angry, and you know you had every right to be. You immediately shot off a reply telling that so-and-so exactly what you thought. Then you regretted it. Byte is Goddess of Angry E-mails. She is the one who sends your fingers flying across the keyboard in answer to that message. Bit is the other goddess of e-mails—the one who says, "Wait." You want to calm down before you send that e-mail. Bit suggests you wait twenty-four hours before answering. Start a draft, save it, and reread it the next day. If you still feel the same, clean it up and send it. Byte is useful in Her place, but always wait a Bit first.

Boudica

Notes:

traditions to be the actual voice of a deity or deified natural element. The next time you are in the presence of this powerful entity, open yourself to the voice or message inherent in this sacred sound; let yourself begin to understand "the voice of thunder," the primal speech of this ancient god.

Sharynne NicMhacha

Notes:

June 3
Sunday

 3rd ♈

Color of the day: Yellow
Incense of the day: Nutmeg

Thunderstorm Meditation

This is the month of thunderstorms in many areas, and the energy of these storms can be sudden and powerful. The ancient Celts worshipped a god called Taranis, "The Thunderer" (much as the name of the Norse God Thor was also associated with thunder). And in some areas of Scotland a folk prayer was made to a powerful deity called "The Voice of Thunder." Thunder is the manifest sound of the potent energies of lightning—fire, light, and movement—and is considered in many

June 4
Monday

 3rd ♈
☽ → ♒ 7:15 pm

Color of the day: White
Incense of the day: Cinnamon

Every Dog has his Day

This is the day to celebrate your magical hound. Dogs don't just accompany dark gods and goddesses on night hunts—they protect their humans and offer unswerving love and devotion. Bless the dog in the name of Cerridwen or Hathor or the

Lady of the Beasts. Take your dog on a long walk. Be completely in the moment with the dog. Don't check your watch. Don't tug the dog away from sniffing or exploring (unless it's putting either one of you in danger). Learn from the dog's appreciation of smell, sight, sound, the delight in the *now* of life and see how you can use the qualities in your own life. Give your dog some favorite treats and a specially blessed meal, and take extra time to play. If you don't have a dog, borrow one!

Cerridwen Iris Shea

Notes:

June 5
Tuesday

 3rd ≈

Color of the day: Scarlet
Incense of the day: Lavender

Resolution Spell

This is a good spell to use to resolve problems that have no clear "right way" or "wrong way."

You'll need a white candle, a green candle, and a red candle. Light the white candle, saying:

> Now I call on the
> Mothers three.
> help me choose.
> hear my plea.

Light the green candle, saying:

> Earth and water,
> Fire and air,
> help me choose
> The path that is fair.

Light the red candle, saying:

> help me do
> What's right for all.
> Upon your wisdom
> I do call.

Let the candles burn out naturally. When the candles burn themselves out, you may find a compromise solution that is workable on all levels. Place the candle drippings in a paper bag and bury it someplace where it won't be disturbed.

Paniteowl

Notes:

June 6
Wednesday

 3rd ≈

Color of the day: Brown
Incense of the day: Ginger

Business Boost Spell

If you own a business, fight dwindling customer levels using a little magic and some aromatherapy. This spell uses incense. Go to a store where you can actually smell what you are buying, and then purchase scents that make you think of prosperity, scents that would make you want to stay in a store and shop. To cast the spell, light a green candle and gently wave your packages of incense over the flame while mentally seeing more customers visiting your business and buying what you have to offer. Allow the candle to burn down. At least once per day for the next week, burn one of the sticks of incense somewhere in your business. Continue to burn them as you feel necessary during those less busy days.

Laurel Reufner

Notes:

June 7
Thursday

 3rd ≈
☽ → ♓ 1:24 am

Color of the day: Turquoise
Incense of the day: Neroli

Financial Trouble Freeze

Bills for hospitals, medications, and accidents can mount up quickly. Only very rarely are these things planned for. This spell can help you to see your way clear through an unexpected financial pothole. Make a photocopy of the bill in question and tear it into small bits. Place the pieces in a clean ice tray. Sprinkle cinquefoil over the tray. As you fill the tray with water, say:

> The obligation is mine,
> but I need more time.
> Go to sleep for now bill,
> until my responsibility I
> can fulfill.
>
> Make it so, make it so!

Place the tray in the freezer until frozen solid. Remove the ice blocks and store them in a plastic bag in the freezer until you can pay the amount in full.

Tammy Sullivan

Notes:

June 8
Friday

3rd ♓
4th quarter 7:43 am

Color of the day: Purple
Incense of the day: Musk

Give Thanks for the Rain

Use this spell to honor the element of water and to encourage rain and fertility in times of drought. In a clear glass bowl, place sea shells and stones associated with the water element, such as moonstone, clear quartz, aquamarine, or a combination of these. Fill the bowl with water. Place floating candles on the water or light an assortment of white, blue, and green candles and place them around the bowl. Remember that water cannot be created. When we honor the element of water, we raise our awareness of the necessity of protecting this sacred resource. Use the water as an offering by pouring it onto a plant when you're finished.

> Water, river, rain,
> and lake,
> help me to know
> what I take.
>
> Ocean, sea, ice,
> and snow,
> Water makes all
> life to grow.

> Grant us wisdom
> in your ways,
> Water to quench us
> all our days.

Ember

Notes:

June 9
Saturday

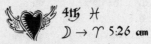
4th ♓
☽ → ♈ 5:26 am

Color of the day: Gray
Incense of the day: Rose

Crystal Sensuality Spell

Crystals can be used for many purposes, including arousing passions, creating romance, and boosting fertility. To enhance your pleasure, create a bath with rose oil and sea salt. Add an emerald or garnet. Soak in the bath for at least thirty minutes. See yourself as a beautiful and desirable goddess or a handsome, strapping god. To help maintain those feelings, carry a pendant of rose quartz, carnelian, kunzite, green and pink tourmaline, or rhodochrosite. For an aphrodisiac effect, scatter a few carnelians or pink tourmalines on the bedside table or nightstand.

Olivia O'Meir

Notes:

close your psychic eyes and ask to see your mind. Open your eyes and imagine healing energy flowing into any areas of your mind that seem unhealthy or uncomfortable. See them fill with healing light. Then close your psychic eyes and ask to see your complete and total being. Open your eyes and see yourself filled to overflowing with beautiful, healthy light that spills out into the world around you.

Kristin Madden

Notes:

June 10
Sunday

 4th ♈

Color of the day: Gold
Incense of the day: Sandalwood

healing the Spirit Visualization

Imagine that you are standing in a room filled with mirrors. Take a good look at yourself and imagine healing energy flowing into any areas that seem unhealthy or uncomfortable. See them fill with healing light. Then close your psychic eyes and ask to see your emotions. Open your eyes and be aware of how your emotions look now. Imagine healing energy flowing into any areas that seem unhealthy or uncomfortable. See them fill with healing light. Then

June 11
Monday

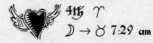 4th ♈
☽ → ♉ 7:29 am

Color of the day: Silver
Incense of the day: Basil

Mater Matuta

Matralia is the Roman holiday for motherly women who have not themselves borne children.

This day honors the aunts, nannies, and other caretakers who make a difference in young people's lives. These women provide a support system for mothers who give birth. Mater Matuta, Goddess of Dawn and Death, oversees this holiday as she is the patron of motherly women and traditionally receives their homage. Today, take time to express your appreciation to a motherly woman—maybe an aunt who helped raise you, or a childless or childfree friend who watches your children sometimes. Seashells, mother-of-pearl jewelry, fish, and other gifts relating to the sea are especially appropriate, as Mater Matuta is also the goddess of harbors and oceans. Nets symbolize connections made by hand, rather than blood; and beautiful glass fishing floats remind us of how motherly women help keep our heads above water!

Elizabeth Barrette

Notes:

June 12
Tuesday

4th ♉

Color of the day: White
Incense of the day: Peony

Anti-Temptation Spell

It's wonderful to indulge, but there are times when indulgence is excessive. Be it chocolate, food, cigarettes, wine, lust, or shopping, most of us experience temptation that lures us from our best intentions. Recognizing the moment when we succumb to temptation is the first step in managing any excess. For example, if your passion is sweet food, next time you crave it take a walk outdoors or clean a drawer or cupboard in your room. If you are at work, have a glass of water or herbal tea or clean out a drawer. Invoke the attributes of the Roman goddess Diana to help you focus on your goals to manage temptation. Ensure that your goals are realistic and break them down into smaller, more achievable ones to help you stay on track. Don't try to give up chocolate altogether; simply reduce your intake so you enjoy it moderation. Replace any feelings of guilt with a positive affirmation such as:

> I respect my body and
> will nurture it with
> exercise every day.

Emely Flak

 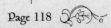

Notes:

Dear Saint Anthony
I pray,
Bring it back
without delay.

Remove the picture of the baby Jesus. Withhold the image of the baby Jesus from Saint Anthony until your lost thing is recovered. Thank Saint Anthony and place both pictures together for at least twenty-four hours.

Lily Gardner

Notes:

June 13
Wednesday

 4th ♉
☽ → ♊ 8:24 am

Color of the day: Yellow
Incense of the day: Poplar

Two Spells to Find Lost Things

Pagans and Christians alike invoke Saint Anthony when something is lost. His feast day is celebrated today. When you've lost your belongings, close your eyes and say:

Dear Saint Anthony,
come around,
Something's lost and
can't be found.

The second spell requires a picture or statue of Saint Anthony and a picture of the baby Jesus. Place the pictures so that the likeness of Saint Anthony can see the likeness of the baby Jesus. Say:

June 14
Thursday
Flag Day

 4th ♊
New Moon 11:13 pm

Color of the day: Green
Incense of the day: Coriander

New Moon Prayer

The Celts used a lunar-based calendar system, and there is a great deal of ancient evidence and modern folklore showing that the

New Moon was the most sacred point of their lunar cycle. Their four holidays would have also taken place in conjunction with the New Moon. The appearance of the crescent New Moon after a sacred period of three dark days and nights was a powerful experience. When you see the New Moon, follow the Celtic tradition by bowing to the Moon and saying the following prayer:

> hail to thee, thou New
> Moon, beautiful guide of
> the stars.
>
> hail to thee, thou New
> Moon, loved one of my
> heart.
>
> If you have found me
> well tonight, seven times
> better may you leave me,
>
> Bright white Moon of
> the seasons, beautiful
> dear one of the skies!

Sharynne NicMhacha

Notes:

June 15
Friday

 1st ♊
☽ → ♋ 9:45 am

Color of the day: Rose
Incense of the day: Sage

Love Poppet Spell

This spell uses seasonal love-attracting flowers that normally bloom in June to bring romance into your life. Gather together the following: red or pink rose petals, wild oxeye daisy flowers, and one leaf and the flowers from a lady's mantle plant. Next, create a simple poppet from pink fabric. Embellish the poppet with the physical characteristics you find attractive in a romantic partner, without thinking of anyone specific. On the lady's mantle leaf write:

> Come to me, lover.

Place the leaf and all the flowers into the poppet and sew it shut with red thread. Pass the poppet through smoke rising from the smoldering foliage of rose geranium. Place the poppet beneath your pillow every night for at least one week as you whisper:

> Come to me, lover.

James Kambos

Notes:

Moonbeams will enchant
and protect your slumber
at night.

May your days be filled
with magic for all of your
life.

Seal this blessing spell with a gentle
kiss on the baby's forehead.

Ellen Dugan

Notes:

June 16
Saturday

 1st ♋

Color of the day: Black
Incense of the day: Nutmeg

Saturday Baby Blessing

As the waxing Moon phase represents birth and new beginnings, this is a perfect time for this magical blessing. Use pink or blue candles, and a natural representation of each of the four elements—perhaps a feather for air, a lava rock for fire, a cup of spring water for the element of water, and a few white rosebuds for the element of earth. Gather the child in your arms and, using the spring water, draw a small star on the baby's forehead. Then say:

We welcome you to this world, our dear little one.

May you have health and wisdom while under the Sun.

June 17
Sunday
Father's Day

 1st ♋
☽ → ♌ 1:25 pm

Color of the day: Amber
Incense of the day: Parsley

Father's Day Meditation

We don't all have our fathers around to celebrate with, and this day becomes a time of contemplation for some of us. Remembrance of your dad is a way to recall his strength and the part he may have played in your life. You can still ask him for blessings or assistance in your life. This is also a day when we can seek healing. We may not have had good relationships with our dads, and remembrance could finally come in the form of forgiveness. Seek closure to a relationship that may not have been the best and move on with your life. We try to remember the good times we had with our fathers and hold on to those moments as bright spots.

Boudica

Notes:

river. Construct paper boats—one for each wish. Draw or paste an image of a dragon on the side of your wish boat. By painting in the pupil in the eye of your dragon, you are awakening him. This is a good time to think of what you want to offer the dragon in your wish boat. A lit votive candle, a small stone, a seed pearl, or a piece of cake are all worthy offerings. The night of June 18, take your wish boat to the banks of a river or a lake and float your wishes to the dragon that lives there.

Lily Gardner

Notes:

June 18
Monday

 1st ♌

Color of the day: Lavender
Incense of the day: Parsley

Spell for Wishes

The earth dragons of Chinese mythology live in lakes and rivers and control the rain, and the annual dragon boat festival takes place around this time. This festival was originally held as a solstice ritual to awaken the dragon gods of the

June 19
Tuesday

 1st ♌
☽ → ♏ 8:45 pm

Color of the day: Red
Incense of the day: Lavender

Recharging Spell

Draw upon the energy of Earth and Sun when you need to

recharge. Gather a tiger's-eye stone, a small container, and some olive oil. Holding the stone in your hand, imagine it glowing from within. Place it in the small container and add enough olive oil to cover it. Set the container in a spot where it will feel the Sun's warmth but not be disturbed, and leave it for seven days. After seven days, remove the stone, wash it gently to remove the oil, and carry it with you. When you need to recharge a bit, hold it gently in your hand and imagine that glow moving up your arm to engulf your body, lending you the stored solar energy.

Laurel Reufner

Notes:

June 20
Wednesday

1st ♏

Color of the day: Topaz
Incense of the day: Frankincense

Spell for the Weary Traveler

Now we begin the summer vacation season. Traveling can be fun, but it can also be stressful. Try this stress-busting ritual to refresh yourself after you arrive at your destination. Travel with some lavender-scented soap or body scrub, witch hazel, and a small pillow to support your neck. Bathe with the lavender soap. Towel off and put on a comfy bathrobe. If possible, refrigerate the witch hazel and apply it to your face with a cotton ball. Massage your temples lightly with the witch hazel and lay down. Rest your head on the small pillow and elevate your feet. Feel all tension draining away; close your eyes and visualize the things you enjoy. Let the images flow. Drift off and take a nap if you wish, resting for at least twenty minutes. When you arise, you'll be ready to enjoy your vacation.

James Kambos

Notes:

June 21
Thursday

Summer Solstice ~ Litha

 1st ♍

☉ → ♋ 2:06 pm

Color of the day: Purple
Incense of the day: Sandalwood

Garden Blessing

Today we celebrate the longest day of the year. In most places, this is the time of summer's most beautiful bounty of flora and fauna. The night is alive with sounds; the air is filled with birdsong. To honor this time of abundance, for now the days will grow shorter, assemble a bouquet of wildflowers, flowers from your garden, or flowers or a plant from a store. Place the flowers or plant somewhere in sight all day. If you don't have a garden of your own, use a plant or flowers to represent the abundance of the season. Focus on the abundance and beauty of the flowers and plants; consider how they were cultivated—where they were grown, and how. Give thanks to farmers and growers for providing for the rest of us, or, if you have a garden of your own, use this blessing to bring abundance:

> Mother Earth,
> thank you for your
> nurturing body,
> the water of your veins,
> the air of your breath.
>
> Father Sun,
> Thank you for your
> warmth.
>
> May this abundant
> season
> bring sweet yield in the
> months to come.
>
> Tonight, we celebrate life!

Ember

Notes:

June 22
Friday

 1st ♍

☽ → ♎ 7:43 am
2nd quarter 9:15 am

Color of the day: White
Incense of the day: Carnation

House Protection Spell

There are numerous protection spells and charms cast between the days of the summer solstice (around June 21) and St. John's Day

(June 24). Using the powers of fire, cast this spell to protect your home from negative energies. Burn thirteen yarrow stalks in your fireplace. When the yarrow has burned down to ash, trace a Star of Solomon with your athame. The Star of Solomon is the six-pointed star made from two triangles that represent harmony. Alternatively, you could make a solar wheel from a willow branch. Divide the wheel with an equal-armed solar cross made of twisted ribbon, cord, or twigs. In the center of the cross attach a small red bag filled with the nine herbs of the "Witches' Charm": mugwort, plantain, watercress, cock-spur grass, chamomile, stinging nettle, apple, thyme, and fennel. Adorn the solar wheel with a sprig of Saint-John's wort and hang it over your front door.

Lily Gardner

Notes:

June 23
Saturday

 2nd ♎

Color of the day: Indigo
Incense of the day: Thyme

Beyond the Labels

Wander slowly around your yard or a park. Walk to anything that attracts you. Give thanks and fully feel your appreciation for whatever this thing is. Name or describe each thing and then ask who or what is beyond the label. Gaze at each thing that attracts your attention and feel what it is like to be in relationship with this thing. Don't label the feeling or imagine it, simply feel how you feel in connection to this object. Continue this with various objects until you feel very relaxed and connected. Ask yourself who you are beyond your labels. Experience anything that comes up without judgment. Open your eyes and see the reflection of yourself in the world around you. What do you see? How does that relate to who you are? What does it teach you? Spend some time being with this experience. Thank the area before leaving.

Kristin Madden

Notes:

June 24
Sunday

 2nd ♎
☽ → ♏ 8:26 pm

Color of the day: Gold
Incense of the day: Lilac

Get the Job Done Spell Bags

Jobs that need to be done sometimes have a way of getting pushed to another time—or maybe there are so many of them you can't figure out where to start. Make a list with the most important things first. Place the list in a spell bag with the following items: quartz crystal for clear thinking, rosemary for remembrance, carnelian to stimulate focus and initiative, and mint for stimulation and energy. Cross each completed job off and return the list to the bag and your pocket. When energy runs low, the smell of the bag should stimulate you, or a brief rest and contemplation of the stones will keep you focused on what remains to be done. Before you know it, that list of jobs will be history.

Boudica

Notes:

June 25
Monday

2nd ♏

Color of the day: Gray
Incense of the day: Cinnamon

Harmonious Home Spell

Keeping the vibrations of one's home harmonious for everyone in it is no easy task, especially if there is more than one child living at home. For this spell you will need a wreath of dried grapevine, a rose quartz stone, fresh gardenia flowers, fresh morning-glory vine, and fresh lavender flowers. Beginning with the morning-glory vine, carefully wind it around and around the grapevine wreath. Place the lavender flowers in the open pockets between the stems. Tie the rose quartz into the center of the wreath with string or ribbon. Twine the gardenias into the wreath last. While you are assembling the wreath, visualize peace and harmony as a beautiful, bright blue sky that floats under your roof. Hang the wreath at eye level in a busy central room. Replace the flowers as needed. You may find it necessary to use florist pins or hot glue to assemble all the ingredients—either one is fine, and won't hurt the effectiveness of the wreath a bit.

Tammy Sullivan

Notes:

Notes:

June 26
Tuesday

2nd ♏

Color of the day: Black
Incense of the day: Chrysanthemum

Goals Spell

With your athame or a knitting needle, write on a large red candle the symbols of things you want to accomplish. If you want to work on your home, a simple drawing of a house will do. If you want to change your habits to improve your health, a Caduceus symbol would be appropriate. If you have a small cauldron, place the candle in it—otherwise a clay bowl will do. Light the candle and focus on the things you want to achieve. Allow the candle to burn out. Promise yourself to do those things necessary to achieve your goal. Leave the candle and bowl (or cauldron) in plain sight until your goals are achieved.

Paniteowl

June 27
Wednesday

2nd ♏
☽ → ♐ 8:23 am

Color of the day: White
Incense of the day: Honeysuckle

Happy Lemonade Spell

Summer is well underway, with most schools releasing children to sunshine, picnics, and fun. Lemonade reminds us of long summer days with good food, laughter, swimming, and leisure—tangy activity followed by the long sweetness of relaxation. Pink lemonade adds the energy of freshness, femininity, and grace. Pour yourself half a glass of lemonade, concentrating on the warmth of the Sun and the joy of long days. Add one ice cube, thinking with intention on the moment when coolness hits you after a hot day. Add a second ice cube and concentrate on the sweetness in your life. Add a third ice cube, concentrating on the magic of summertime. Gaze at this concoction of magical relaxation. Drink with intention, bringing the energy of summertime, relaxation, sweetness, and coolness into your life. Then go outside and have some fun!

Gail Wood

Notes:

June 28
Thursday

 2nd ♐

Color of the day: Green
Incense of the day: Eucalyptus

**A Spell to Protect
Your Book of Shadows**

This is a spell that will protect and bless your Book of Shadows. In this waxing Moon phase you can visualize the pages of your book growing thick with wisdom and witchery. Set the book up on your work space, light a few candles, get your favorite incense going, and set a magical mood. Now ground and

center yourself. Raise your energy high, and then hold your hands palms down over the book. Repeat the charm while you empower the book with the powers of the four elements, knowledge, wisdom, and illumination.

> As the Moon does
> grow fuller and fuller
> each night,
> My Book of Shadows
> grows too, in
> knowledge and light.
>
> By earth, air, sky,
> and sea, as above
> now so below,
> The elemental powers
> spin and my magic holds.

Ellen Dugan

Notes:

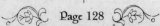

June 29
Friday

2nd ♐
☽ → ♑ 6:05 pm

Color of the day: Pink
Incense of the day: Geranium

Inanna Blessing

Today is Friday, the day dedicated to the goddess of love. This calls for a time to invoke the Mesopotamian love goddess Inanna for passion, courage, and confidence. Inanna is also known as the queen of heaven and goddess of war and fertility. Prepare an altar to honor Inanna with her fertility symbol of dates. The eight-pointed star is also one of her symbols. Draw an eight-pointed star on a piece of paper or cardboard and place the dates at the center. Sit at your altar, eat one of the dates, and imagine your life blessed with the energy of Inanna, filling you with confidence and courage to attract positive outcomes and passion in your life. As you eat, say these words:

> Goddess Inanna,
> As I eat your sacred
> fruit of dates
> From your symbol of
> radiant light,
> I ask for your blessings
> for confidence
> On this Friday night.

> Emely Flak

Notes:

June 30
Saturday

2nd ♑
Full Moon 9:49 am

Color of the day: Brown
Incense of the day: Sandalwood

Moonstone Scrying

Fill a black cauldron or a dark ceramic or glass bowl with clear water. Place a cleansed and consecrated moonstone in it. Light a white candle and keep it nearby. Sit either outside or near a window that has the light of the Full Moon coming through it. Ground, center, and quiet your mind. Ask a simply-phrased question and use the moonstone water to scry your answer. Take your time: you're working with the water and the unconscious. The images will swirl and form and mutate; don't try to make them be anything—let them be what they are. Make sure to write down both

the question and the information
revealed in detail. Dry the moonstone
and cauldron thoroughly after use.

Cerridwen Iris Shea

Notes:

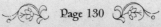

July is the seventh month of the year. Its astrological sign is Cancer, the crab (June 21–July 22), a cardinal water sign ruled by the Moon. July is the month of the ripening. In orchards, fields, and gardens, nature moves toward the miracle of the harvest. In July heat, the Goddess fulfills her promise and oversees maturing crops. The Summer Solstice has passed, but nature pulses with life. Hummingbirds flash among the bee balm, and mint varieties spread like wildfire. Water is an important magical element in July. Birds refresh themselves in birdbaths. Thunder rumbles on hot afternoons, bringing a promise of rain. Dragonflies skim the surface of ponds, and vacationers head to the shore. Salt water and seashells are good ways to include the element of water in any rituals now. Independence Day, July 4, is the major holiday of high summer. Not only can we celebrate our nation's independence, we can also use give thanks for July's abundance, which will sustain us during the coming months. We are blessed with richness in July, perhaps the reason the old ones referred to July's Full Moon as the Blessing Moon. Magic during this Moon may include all forms of prosperity charms. When you cast a spell now, you will feel the vitality of the earth.

July 1
Sunday

 3rd ♑

Color of the day: Yellow
Incense of the day: Juniper

Life's Lessons Spell

The mysteries of life, death, and rebirth are central to modern-day Witches, offering many us life lessons. While it is easy to honor life and rebirth, we also need to honor and recognize death and sacrifice. Take time to reflect in a simple ritual. You will need a tarot deck, mugwort incense, a black candle, some paper to record your thoughts, and a safe, private space. Invoke a goddess of truth, such as Maat or Hecate:

> Goddess guide my sight.
> Show me on
> this very night
> The lessons that
> I have learned
> So I will not make
> the same turn.

Shuffle the tarot deck and turn over three cards. They will show you the lessons your mind, body, and soul have learned. Make notes and repeat the spread as many times you need to. When finished reading, say:

> Goddess, I thank you on
> this night
> For the gift of
> clear sight.

> I know life is a
> great adviser,
> And it makes me so
> much wiser.

Olivia O'Meir

Notes:

Holiday lore: Today is the first day of the season for climbing Mt. Fuji in Yamabiraki, Japan. Mt. Fuji is the highest peak in Japan and is revered in Japanese culture. Considered the foremother or grandmother of Japan, Fuji is an ancient fire goddess of the indigenous Ainu people. In modern times, the Ainu mostly resided on the northern island of Hokkaido. The name *Fuji* was derived from an Ainu word that means "fire" or "deity of fire." Each year since the Meiji era, a summer festival has been held to proclaim the beginning of the climbing season and to pray for the safety of local inhabitants and visitors or pilgrims to the sacred mountain. The two-month climbing season begins today, and ends on August 30.

July 2
Monday

 3rd ♑
☽ → ♒ 1:24 am

Color of the day: Lavender
Incense of the day: Sage

Protection Blessing for an Expectant Mother

Today is the Festival for Expectant Mothers. Use this auspicious day to prepare a special Witches' Ladder for a mother-to-be. Use a red cord the height of the mother. Knot the cord nine times, inserting one of the following charms into each knot: carnelian, amber, coral, rose quartz, a sprig of lavender, a sprig of chamomile, apple seeds, a charm in the shape of a heart, and a charm in the shape of a baby. As you make each knot say:

> Bona Dea, make her strong,
> Bona Dea, keep her safe.
> An easy delivery,
> A healthy child.
> Bless this mother and her baby.

When each knot is tied, kiss the knot and go to the next one. When you are finished with the ladder, pass it through the smoke from a fire made of motherwort.

Lily Gardner

Notes:

July 3
Tuesday

 3rd ♒

Color of the day: Red
Incense of the day: Myrrh

Energy Restoration Potion

Searing hot temperatures have a way of sapping the energy right out from one's body. The following energy potion can help replace this lost energy. Brew pinches of mint and ginseng herbs along with a green tea bag. Steep for three minutes. Strain and serve over ice with lemon slices for a refreshing tonic. In addition, you may wish to take Solomon's seal, Gotu Kola, and myrrh herbal supplement tablets to rev up flagging energy levels. Once restored, seal the energy inside the body by taking a cool shower and rubbing a rosewater and glycerin solution into wet skin. As you do so, visualize the energy vibrating just below the skin's surface. Carry this vision with you throughout the day. Most importantly, make sure to drink plenty of water to keep the body hydrated and functioning at its highest level.

Tammy Sullivan

Notes:

of our servicemen and servicewomen who are at home or on foreign soil. Ask blessings on those who have served our country in the past and those who will serve in the future. Circle the flag with a censer, saying:

> By the colors that wave
> over land and sea,
> I send my wish that all
> may be free.

Paniteowl

Notes:

July 4
Wednesday
Independence Day

 3rd ≈
☽ → ♓ 6:52 am

Color of the day: Brown
Incense of the day: Evergreen

Spell to Preserve Freedom
Cast a circle, and in the center place a U.S. flag. At the four cardinal points, place three sparklers and a copy of the Declaration of Independence. Light the sparklers at sundown, and as they burn invoke your deities. Ask them for protection and support of all who defend the ideals of our country. Read the Declaration of Independence out loud. Ask that the deities protect all

Holiday notes: On July 4, 1776, the Second Continental Congress adopted the Declaration of Independence. Philadelphians were first to mark the anniversary of American independence with a celebration, but Independence Day became commonplace only after the War of 1812. By the 1870s, the Fourth of July was the most important secular holiday in the country, celebrated even in far-flung communities on the western frontier of the country.

July 5
Thursday

 3rd ♓

Color of the day: Turquoise
Incense of the day: Cedar

Gloom Removal Spell

The waning Moon is the perfect time to remove what you no longer need from your life. Light a black candle. Make a list of all the things that make you feel sad, depressed, or defeated. Let yourself fully experience these emotions. Now, beside each negative list a positive step to counteract or remove the negative. Once you do so, draw a line through the negative, setting the positive counteraction into motion. Burn the list in a flameproof container and get moving, taking the positive steps you listed.

Cerridwen Iris Shea

Notes:

July 6
Friday

 3rd ♓
☽ → ♈ 10:56 am

Color of the day: White
Incense of the day: Musk

Beauty Purification

In the evening, draw a warm bath and add several drops of rosemary and lavender essential oils, or use dried herbs and wrap them in cheesecloth and toss the bag into the water. Burn frankincense and a green candle in the room. As you bathe, visualize the water cleansing away negative energy; feel it renewing your skin and your spirits. Feel your inner beauty being set free by the power of the water. Chant:

> Water pure, cleanse
> and renew,
> Take the old away
> with you.
> Rinse me clean with
> beauty true,
> Leave inner glow
> shining through.

After bathing, apply tea-tree lotion to your skin and get a restful night's sleep.

Ember

Notes:

July 7
Saturday

 3rd ♈
4th quarter 12:53 pm

Color of the day: Blue
Incense of the day: Ylang-ylang

Release Your Limitations Spell

This fire release is based on a Vaishnava tradition and is a powerful method for releasing all that you no longer want in your life. Build and light a fire in your fireplace or in a fireproof container such as a cauldron. Taking up a handful of grain, sit in meditation before the fire. As you gaze into the fire, bring to mind all those issues, patterns, or situations that you want to let go of. Allow all the feelings and memories that these limitations evoke to be experienced. Send each of these into the grain in your hand. When you are ready, throw the grain into the fire, chanting:

> holy grain, I give to thee
> My challenges
> to be set free.
> Sacred Fire of
> transformation
> Cleanse and clear
> my limitations.

Kristin Madden

Notes:

July 8
Sunday

 4th ♈
☽ → ♉ 1:54 pm

Color of the day: Orange
Incense of the day: Pine

Aromatherapy Stress Relief

In today's world, stress is a major health issue. Learn to leave your work at your workplace. Even if you work at home, close the door to your workspace or just turn off the light at the desk where you work and walk away from it. Separate work from home. Find a fragrance to use in your house that says work is done and this is the place to relax. Have this fragrance on hand as you make time after work to relax and unwind. Do this every day. Soon the smell alone will trigger a response that will tell your body it's time to shed the stress and relax.

Boudica

Notes:

July 9
Monday

 4th ♉

Color of the day: White
Incense of the day: Pine

Protection Against Disappearing Items

If you have ever been in a situation where personal items disappear from your desk, your room, or your bathroom, then this spell for protection against mysterious disappearance or theft is for you. When you are away from the place you wish to protect, shield it with an often-used sign of protection: the eye. On a piece of cardboard, either draw two eyes or paste two eyes cut out from a magazine. Draw the shape of a masquerade-ball mask around the eyes with a thick felt marker and cut it out. Make as many as necessary to place in drawers, in bags, or on your desk. This spell uses that feeling of being watched that occurs when we are in a room or gallery with photographs or paintings that feature people with prominent eyes.

Emely Flak

Notes:

July 3
Tuesday

 4th ♉
D → ♊ 4:10 pm

Color of the day: Black
Incense of the day: Clove

Hummingbird Spell

The element of air represents the mind, speed, and ephemeral beauty. Jewels associated with air include amethyst, yellow fluorite, and clear quartz. Scents include frankincense and lavender. The colors of air are white, clear, yellow, and pale blue. One excellent way to commune with air is to hang a hummingbird feeder. Hummers are among the most beautiful birds, like living gems. They dart about the garden with the speed of thought. Choose a red feeder, the hummingbirds' favorite color. Fill with a commercial nectar blend, or get a recipe for sugar-water from a conservation site. Don't use honey or food coloring. To help the birds find your feeder quickly, visualize it as a huge red flower amidst a cloud of hummingbirds, and say this as you hang it:

> Hummingbirds so swift
> and fair
> Teach me all the gifts
> of air.

In return I bid you eat
Of this scarlet flower
sweet.

Elizabeth Barrette

Notes:

Notes:

July 11
Wednesday

 4th ♊

Color of the day: Topaz
Incense of the day: Maple

Travel Simplicity Spell

Send those travel complica-
tions packing with this simple
charm. On a piece of paper, write
down all the things that are holding
up your travel plans. Try to use ink
that you know to be water soluble
(it's fine if you don't have any, but
it will make the visualization in the
next part easier). Take your list to
a nearby sink and hold it under the
running water, visualizing all your
problems going down the drain along
with the water.

Laurel Reufner

July 12
Thursday

4th ♊
☽ → ♋ 6:39 pm

Color of the day: Purple
Incense of the day: Maple

honeysuckle prosperity Spell

Begin this spell on a Thursday
evening and repeat it nightly
for one week. Place two green
candles upon your altar and surround
them with honeysuckle stems and
flowers. Light the candles and meditate on your money needs while you
inhale the floral scent of the honeysuckle. Sprinkle ground nutmeg over
the burning candles to "feed" the fire
elements and to act as an offering.
On the seventh night, crumble the
honeysuckle, which should be dry by
now, into your cauldron, and ignite it
with one of the burning candles.

Sprinkle nutmeg over the cauldron and say:

> For seven nights I have performed this spell. Let money come to me in the most perfect way. Only time will tell.

James Kambos

Notes:

of swirling, turbulent energy. See the energetic thoughts of others spin, noticing the contours, textures, and boundaries. Next, move swiftly and strongly underneath the boundaries. Cross the border of ill-luck and fear into the world of the magic of thirteen. Move into this world, noticing the magic, power, and symbolism of this powerful, lucky day. Breathe in that magic and power as you come back into your space.

Gail Wood

Notes:

July 13
Friday

 4th ☽
Color of the day: Rose
Incense of the day: Jasmine

Meditation on Friday the 13th
Thirteen is a strong, powerful number, indivisible by any other number. Branded unlucky in almost every tradition, the number has strong esoteric meanings as well. When the day falls on Friday, people feel this is a day of insurmountable ill luck. To boldly find the true magic of the day, go into a deep meditative state and find yourself in the midst

July 14
Saturday

4th ☽
New Moon 8:04 am
☽ → ♌ 10:43 pm

Color of the day: Brown
Incense of the day: Nutmeg

Banishing Unwanted Attention
Sometimes we need to get rid of some unwanted attention, or we're getting a little too much atten-

tion. Gather a small handful of clover, a black candle, and a mirror for this simple spell. Working at dark, by candlelight, slowly drop the clover onto the surface of the mirror while visualizing yourself being invisible to those whose attentions you would like to avoid. Allow the candle to burn down completely and it is done. Afterward, place the mirror on your altar or other safe place.

Laurel Reufner

Notes:

breaths. You're standing at the edge of a lush forest. It is twilight, a time of great magic. Walk into the forest. You are safe and warm. Walk the path until you reach a circle with a fire in the center. Approach the bookstand you see on the other side. Open the book and begin reading. Your new name will either be on the pages of the book or someone will speak it. After you receive your name, say "Thank you." Begin walking back down the path. When you reach the forest edge, open your eyes. You are now awake and grounded, knowing your new name.

Olivia O'Meir

Notes:

July 15
Sunday

 1st ♌

Color of the day: Gold
Incense of the day: Lavender

New Name Meditation

This spell finds someone a new name. The ingredients for this spell include one white candle and small pouch of herbs. Use herbs for dreams, meditation, and inspiration, like lavender and mugwort. Close your eyes and take some deep

July 16
Monday

1st ♌

Color of the day: Gray
Incense of the day: Basil

Ocean Retreat Spell

Visit the ocean at this time of year to experience its

powerful cooling waters and honor its sacred essence. A return to the salt waters of our creation can be a potent healing and transformational experience. In Scotland, the ocean was believed to be so powerful that it could take in and transmute disease. A charm was used in which part of the illness was given "to the great surging sea, for the ocean itself is the best instrument to carry it." Make a prayer to the Irish god of the sea, Mannanán mac Lir, or to the British divine healer Morgan le Fay (whose name means "Born of the Sea"). Make an offering (an object, or a pledge to help heal the oceans) before asking for their deep healing.

Sharynne NicMhacha

Notes:

July 17
Tuesday

  1st ♌
      ☽ → ♍ 5:39 am

Color of the day: Scarlet
Incense of the day: Poplar

Butterfly Wishing Spell

Butterflies are perfect for wishing magic. Take a walk in a butterfly garden, watching them gracefully flit about from flower to flower seeking nectar. Take your time in selecting which butterfly you want to carry your wish skyward. Wait until it has landed on a flower and then make your wish, knowing that when the butterfly takes off once more, your wish will be carried away with it.

Laurel Reufner

Notes:

July 18
Wednesday

 1st ♏

Color of the day: White
Incense of the day: Musk

Traveling Spell Bags

When traveling by plane, boat, or train, luggage can be misplaced. Put a spell bag of comfrey root and oregano in your luggage to ensure it will arrive when you do. Carrying a piece of moldavite (green translucent meteorites) or turquoise protects travelers. A spell bag containing feverfew can ward against sickness or accident during travel. Copper bracelets are said to aid against motion sickness. Make a mixture of salt, pine needles, and lavender to spread on the floor in hotel rooms to draw away negativity and the energy from former occupants. This mix will not set off the smoke alarms as smudge might.

Boudica

Notes:

July 19
Thursday

 1st ♏

☽ → ♎ 3:53 pm

Color of the day: Crimson
Incense of the day: Chrysanthemum

Isis Spell for a Long and Healthy Life

Today is the celebration of Isis's birthday. Isis defeated death to bring back her beloved husband, Osiris. She promised her followers that if they prayed to her, she could prolong their lives into old age. Begin this spell by making a corn cake for Isis:

1 1/4 cups flour
3/4 cup yellow cornmeal
4 tsp. baking powder
1/2 tsp. salt
1/4 cup sugar
1 egg
1 cup milk
1 tbsp. melted butter

Mix ingredients and pour into a buttered 8-inch baking pan. Bake in a 425° oven for 20 minutes. When the cake is finished, light a fire you have prepared for this spell. Break off bits of the cake and feed them into the fire, asking Isis to grant you a long and healthy life. Using a feather, fan the smoke so it covers your body.

Lily Gardner

Notes:

plate, then repeat the charm three times.

> Yemaya, I hold your
> offering within my
> hands.
> Send rain gently to the
> Earth, bringing life to
> the land.

If the melon is gone in the morning, know that your request will soon be answered.

Ellen Dugan

Notes:

July 20
Friday

1st ♎

Color of the day: Pink
Incense of the day: Chrysanthemum

A Spell to Bring Rain

This spell calls on Yemaya, mother goddess of the oceans and bringer of life-giving rains. Correspondences for Yemaya include seashells, blue and white glass beads, coral, turquoise stones, and white or blue flowers. Yemaya is envisioned as a beautiful black mermaid. If you leave her a traditional offering of sliced melon and make a sincere request for rain, she will answer you within forty-eight hours. Take a plate of melon slices outside in the evening and arrange a few of Yemaya's correspondences around them. Make the set-up pretty, and take a moment to visualize this ancient goddess. Place your hands on either side of the

July 21
Saturday

1st ♎

Color of the day: Indigo
Incense of the day: Ginger

Feng Shui Cleansing Spell

Have you ever worked or lived in a place where there has been an argument or conflict? Even after the discord has settled, there is a residue of disruptive energy. You can clear this space to restore balance and energy flow based on the principles of feng shui and magic. Find a bell or two sticks that make a sharp noise when struck together. Walk through the affected space and ring the bell or clap the two sticks in each corner of the room to shift stale energy. Imagine the energy moving freely again as you do this. Light a stick of frankincense incense to complete the cleansing. If you are clearing an area at work, check first to see if the burning of incense is permitted. This ritual can also be carried out when moving into a new home or office.

Emely Flak

Notes:

Color of the day: Amber
Incense of the day: Violet

Harmony Spell

Cloves are a potent herb to halt gossip, malicious talk, and slander. Oranges bring love and luck. Using one whole thin-skinned orange and some whole cloves, create a pomander by sticking a large quantity of cloves into the orange. Mix together small quantities of orris root (protection), cinnamon (healing), and nutmeg (fidelity), and a small quantity of lemon or orange oil (clarity and purity). Roll the clove-studded orange in the mixture and then wrap it in mesh, tissue, or cheesecloth fabric. Tie with a pink ribbon, creating a hanging loop. Decorate it and make it a lovely ornament. Hang the pomander in a room where arguments happen or in a closet with clothes that are worn in difficult situations. Let harmony prevail!

Gail Wood

Notes:

July 23
Monday

 2nd ♏

☉ → ♌ 1:00 am

Color of the day: Silver
Incense of the day: Coriander

Lassie Come home Spell

Here is a spell to help you locate a lost pet. Take a silver candle and engrave your pet's name along the side. Set the candle in a holder and then light it. As the candle begins to burn, envision your pet wearing a silver collar and leash. Now in your mind's eye gently give the leash a tug and gather it back in toward you, silently calling your pet home. Repeat the following chant while you visualize your pet coming back to you.

> What once was lost,
> now is found,
> As my magic
> circles round.
> Lady, send my pet home
> safely to me,
> And as I will it, then so
> shall it be.

> Ellen Dugan

Notes:

July 24
Tuesday

 2nd ♏

☽ → ♐ 4:29 pm

Color of the day: White
Incense of the day: Gardenia

The Protection of Mars

Tuesday belongs to Mars. Relevant concerns include power, protection, warfare, and masculinity. The color of Mars is red—or rust, as from iron, which is the metal associated with this planet. Stones include ruby, garnet, and red jasper. Scents include dragon's blood, ginger, and myrrh. Protection à la Mars is the kind that believes the best defense is a good offense. Use this spell to guard yourself in a competitive work environment, rough sports, or other combative arenas where gentler protections would not suit. You'll need your athame and a pinch of dragon's blood. Sprinkle the red powder over the blade and say:

> Opponents beware!
> I come
> With bright blade and
> beating drum
> To conquer all that I see.

> My sword and my shield
> swing free;
> I give as good as I get.

You can't win;
I'll beat you yet!

Whenever you feel threatened, visualize your athame parrying all attacks.

Elizabeth Barrette

Notes:

heard. See them standing to applaud you, smiling and cheering. You have delivered a fantastic speech that the audience will never forget. See them thanking you afterward and shaking your hand. Carry this stone with you any time you face a situation where communication could be a challenge.

Ember

Notes:

July 25
Wednesday

 2nd ♐

Color of the day: Yellow
Incense of the day: Gardenia

Quartz Communication Spell

Use a piece of citrine quartz or other golden yellow stone. First, cleanse the stone by holding it under running water for a few seconds. Focus your intent on clearing the stone of any negative energy. Next, charge this stone with purpose. Close your fingers around the stone and visualize yourself speaking in front of a large audience. They are mesmerized by your eloquence and intelligence. They understand everything you say. Your message is

July 26
Thursday

2nd ♐

Color of the day: Green
Incense of the day: Neroli

Cinnamon Coffee Money Spell

Brew a special blend this morning and attract abundant money to you all day long. In an electric coffeemaker, fill the filter with your usual amount of favorite ground coffee. Then add a touch of cinnamon, about a quarter teaspoon per cup. Smell deeply of the mix and allow the delicious aroma to fill your senses.

Coffee dark and
coffee rich,

Bless this humble
Kitchen Witch.

Cinnamon, sweet wood
from across the sea,
Bring free and abundant
money to me.

Turn on the coffeemaker and get ready for your day. As the heat releases the flavors, it fills the water with your intent. The steam carries this energy to the God and Goddess and, as you drink, your energy field attunes to the manifestation of this spell.

Kristin Madden

Notes:

delightful scent. Dab the oil on light bulbs, linens, and pulse points. Take a hot bubble bath, scatter rose petals around the room, light a few pink and red candles and—voila!—you are ready for a romantic evening. To make the oil, grind the following herbs in your mortar and pestle: red and pink rose petals (passion and romance), hibiscus petals (passion), and cardamom seeds (love and passion). Add a pinch of vanilla extract (love) and apple fragrance oil (love). Just one drop of the fragrance oil will be plenty, so be careful not to overdo it. Activate the magical properties by whispering the oil's function to it. Relax and allow the oil to fulfill its task.

Tammy Sullivan

Notes:

July 27
Friday

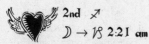 2nd ♐
☽ → ♑ 2:21 am

Color of the day: Coral
Incense of the day: Evergreen

Recipe for Romance

Aromatic herbal oils add subtle vibrations to the atmosphere while filling entire rooms with

July 28
Saturday

2nd ♑

Color of the day: Black
Incense of the day: Parsley

Totem Animal Spell

Now would be a good time to get in touch with your totem animals so that you will be able to see the world in a much larger perspective. Pay close attention and write in a notebook all the animals that you see during one week of midsummer. Contact with your totem animal can come in a variety of ways: through an article in a book, or a program on TV, or simply walking around in your own backyard. Once you have a list of these animals, do your homework. Research the animals' characteristics and habits. You will find that you will become aware of situations you need to know about through the intervention of your totem animal. Allow nature to help you understand your life.

Paniteowl

Notes:

July 29
Sunday

2nd ♑

☽ → ♒ 9:13 am

🌕 Full Moon 8:48 pm

Color of the day: Yellow
Incense of the day: Cedar

Blessing Moon Spell

The old-timers knew July's Full Moon as the Blessing Moon, because this is the time when Mother Earth begins to bless us with her richness. The monarda and tall garden phlox fill the flower bed with a heavenly fragrance. Tomatoes fatten and the corn tassels out. By day the hummingbird dashes from flower to flower; by night the mysterious sphinx moth haunts the garden border sipping nectar. At night above the ripening fields, the Blessing Moon of July rises. She glows like a copper disk, shining with a warmth like no other Full Moon. Honor her beginning at dusk. On your altar place as many vases of flowers as you wish. Burn burgundy and green candles. Fill a clear glass bowl with spring water; stir in a clockwise direction with your finger. Carry the bowl outdoors, or at least to a window where you can view the Moon. Raise the bowl until you can see the Blessing Moon through the water and speak these words:

You who have been
known by many names,
and have shed your light
on our Earth since time
began, bless us with the
bounty of the field and
the vine.

Gently swirl the bowl while gazing at
the shimmering moonlight. In simple
ritual, respectfully pour the water
onto the Earth. Pause and be aware
of the summer night—the stars, the
crickets, and the fireflies.

James Kambos

Notes:

outside and ground and center. Hold
it up to the skies, saying,

Goddess of night,
Goddess of bright,
Speak to me in
A shower of light.

Look up at the sky and celebrate the
heavens. After some time with the
charts, lie back and let your own patterns form in the sky. See what possibilities you can divine, what portents
the patterns in the stars hold.

Cerridwen Iris Shea

Notes:

July 30
Monday

3rd ≈

Color of the day: Ivory
Incense of the day: Poplar

Stargazer Spell

Go to the children's section
of your favorite bookstore.
Purchase a basic star chart (astro-
nomical, not astrological). Take it

July 31
Tuesday

3rd ≈
☽ → ♓ 1:40 pm

Color of the day: Red
Incense of the day: Lavender

Honoring Lugh

The evening of July 31 is the
beginning of the Celtic holiday
known as Lughnasadh (the Feast of

the God Lugh). In Christian times, it was called Lammas (Anglo-Saxon for "Loaf Mass"). It has always been a special holiday for me, as it is my birthday! Lugh instituted this sacred time to honor his foster mother Tailtiu, who cleared the land in preparation for agriculture. Various divine women were honored at this time in Ireland, including Lugh's wives Naas and Bui, the sorceress Carmun, and the goddess Macha. These goddesses seem to have given their lives or energies in order for the land to prosper. Thousands of years later, we can invoke their sacred names once more and make an offering of first fruits or a sacred loaf, lighting a flame in remembrance of their sacrifice.

Sharynne NicMhacha

Notes:

August is the eighth month of the year and is named for Augustus Caesar. Its astrological sign is Leo the lion (July 22–August 23), a fixed fire sign ruled by the Sun. In August we are surrounded by the power and glory of the Goddess. The fields of August bring forth bounty. In nature, yellow and gold dominate with corn, sunflowers, black-eyed Susans, and goldenrod brightening the landscape. The month begins with Lammas, or Lughnasadh, the first of the harvest sabbats. Grains are honored now, and breads are always found on the Lammas table. Nowadays, attending a county fair is a pleasant way to observe the harvest season. Produce, canned foods, and baked goods are proudly displayed along with prize ribbons. In August you can occasionally feel the breath of autumn. There's a coolness in the breeze, and a change in the angle of the sunlight, which reminds us summer is not endless. At twilight, the katydid begins scratching its late summer song. The ancient Romans held Diana's feast day on August 13. It was a time of feasting and enjoying the farmer's bounty. Many Native Americans celebrated the corn harvest in August. This festival eventually gave August's Full Moon its name: the Corn Moon. Magic for the Corn Moon may focus on health, fertility, or abundance.

August 1
Wednesday
Lammas

3rd ♓

Color of the day: Brown
Incense of the day: Ginger

Sacred Feast of Lughnasadh

Celebrate the Celtic festival of the first harvest called Lammas in a simple and homey way. Display and cook with seasonal veggies and fruits from your garden or picked up fresh from the market. Make a pretty centerpiece out of sunflowers; arrange them in a sturdy vase. Try arranging some glossy red or golden-yellow apples in a wooden bowl. Bake up a loaf of whole-wheat bread, drizzle it with honey, and share it with your family or coven. Light a golden candle and stop and take a moment to reflect and to honor this sabbat with this charm:

> Lammas, the celebration
> of the first harvest,
> Abundance, joy, and
> prosperity I now request.
>
> May the Earth's many
> blessings flow upon us,
> May my loved ones
> prosper and enjoy success.

Ellen Dugan

Notes:

Holiday lore: Lammas is a bittersweet holiday, mingling joy at the current high season's harvest with the knowledge that summer is soon at an end. Many cultures have "first fruit" rituals on this day—the Celt's version is called Lughnasadh; the Anglo-Saxon version called Hlafmasse. In the Middle Ages, the holiday settled on August 1, taking its current form for the most part, with sheaves of wheat and corn blessed on this day.

August 2
Thursday

3rd ♓
☽ → ♈ 4:43 pm

Color of the day: Turquoise
Incense of the day: Coriander

Carmun Pledge

In early Ireland a great gathering took place at harvest time which lasted for seven days. This was known as the Feast of Carmun, who was a beautiful sorceress (as well as an experienced warrior). Each of the seven days was consecrated to a certain group of people: the first day for holy people, the second for high kings, the third for women, and so on. People made a solemn pledge to hold the fair every three years, swearing by the elements to never forget to hold the gathering. Holding the fair was believed to ensure "grain, milk, peace and happy ease, full nets and ocean's abundance." Make a pledge to always give thanks for the earth's bounty:

> By the sea and all its
> creatures,
> By the skies and the
> bountiful Earth,
> With all my senses and
> all I possess
> I honor the abundance of
> the land.

Sharynne NicMhacha

Notes:

August 3
Friday

3rd ♈

Color of the day: White
Incense of the day: Dill

Crystal Clarity Spell

Those we love are more likely to bear our tempers and experience us when we are at our worst. Tongue-lashings, moodiness, and fussy or whiny behavior are examples of the abuse we sometimes heap upon our partners, friends, and family. This spell helps us to see when we are hurting those we care about so that we can change destructive behavior. Take a yellow candle and place it in the center of a circle of agate chunks and honeysuckle flowers. Light the candle and gaze into the flame. Say:

Flame, lend your light so
that I may see.
Stones, bring me
clarity. honeysuckle
scent, such a delight,
lend me your sweet-
ness to gift to loved ones
tonight. I call these
things unto me, as I
speak it, so mote it be!

Tammy Sullivan

Notes:

to enjoy the sense of place. Breathe
deeply, give thanks, and let yourself
truly relax. Spend the next few hours
reading, writing, and sipping. Let a
single afternoon refresh you as much
as a week at a spa!

Cerridwen Iris Shea

Notes:

August 4
Saturday

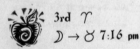 3rd ♈
☽ → ♉ 7:16 pm

Color of the day: Gray
Incense of the day: Rose

Lazy hazy Summer Spell
This is a perfect spell to do in a
hammock. (If you don't have
a hammock, any relaxing place will
do.) Take your journal, a pen, a
book, and your favorite beverage to
a place you can relax, uninterrupted,
for a few hours. Take a few minutes

August 5
Sunday

 3rd ♉
4th quarter 5:19 pm

Color of the day: Orange
Incense of the day: Patchouli

Wishing on a Star
The warm nights of August give
us an opportunity to remember our childhood. There's nothing
wrong with using an old rhyme and
wishing upon a star to make our
dreams come true. Before the Sun
sets, take a blanket and lie comfortably where you can watch the first
star appear in the night sky. Think
about your fondest desire. Think
about what you will need to do in

order to make that dream come true. As the first star appears, recite the old poem:

> Star bright, star light,
> first star I see tonight.
> I wish I may,
> I wish I might,
> Make my dream
> Come true tonight.

Make a wish to truly find a way to accomplish your dream.

Paniteowl

Notes:

August 6
Monday

 4th ♉
☽ → ♊ 10:01 pm

Color of the day: Lavender
Incense of the day: Cinnamon

Peace Meditation

This is Hiroshima Peace Day, commemorating those who died when the nuclear bombs were dropped on Japan and calling for peace throughout the world. By joining your own search for peace with all those throughout the world, you create strong magic. Breathe deeply into the center of your being. Connect your energy with the Mother Earth, breathing in her love and compassion. Center your awareness on your inner being and use her energy to purify places within you that are in conflict. Patiently and lovingly move and transform your inner wars into peaceful energy. Breathe deeply and fill yourself with a clear violet light, and move it out of your crown into the universe. Feel your loving, peaceful energy meld with the others who are working for peace. Breathe deeply and pray for peace everywhere.

Gail Wood

Notes:

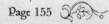

August 7
Tuesday

 4th ♊

Color of the day: Scarlet
Incense of the day: Maple

Birthday Spell

Use this spell today or on the day you celebrate your birth. The old saying goes: "A year older, a year wiser." Focus on the wisdom of your years. Welcome the growth and change and know that all things age. Don't worry about the aging of the body. Visualize the radiant inner beauty you possess manifesting within and without you. Light a candle—or use birthday candles on a cake—and chant:

> I'm older than I've
> ever been
> But younger than I'll
> ever be;
> Wiser than I've
> ever been,
> Yet more learning waits
> for me.

> Age will touch the
> body but
> Inner beauty reigns.
> It shines through me
> despite the years,
> My youthful spirit still
> remains.

Ember

Notes:

August 8
Wednesday

4th ♊

Color of the day: White
Incense of the day: Juniper

Computer Protection Spell

Computers are portals to other realms. Like windows or doors, a computer gives us access to the outside world. And like any other opening, they should be protected so negativity can't enter. To protect your computer from any gremlins which may be lurking, purify your work area with a Native American–style smudge stick. A cedar and sage combination is good. Or smolder rosemary and thyme in a heat-proof dish. Whatever you use, after the smoke begins to rise, wave the smoke over your computer with a white feather. Between ritual cleansings keep a small dish of white sage by your computer; it will help deter bad vibrations.

James Kambos

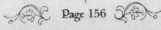

Notes:

to sprinkle lightly onto resumes, job applications, and cover letters before sending them out.

Laurel Reufner

Notes:

August 9
Thursday

 4th ♊
☽ → ♋ 1:36 am

Color of the day: Green
Incense of the day: Sandalwood

Just That Little Extra Spell

This spell will help you find a job, not a career. This is for those seeking something to keep them afloat while looking for a career, or perhaps they need a little something extra to make ends meet. You will need the want ads, a green candle, and a mix of cumin, cinnamon, ginger, and nutmeg. The spices can be already powdered, or you can powder them during the spellcasting. Place the want ads somewhere safe near the candle and then light the candle. Stir together the spice mixture as you focus on earning extra money. After it is thoroughly mixed together, store it in a special jar. Use

August 10
Friday

4th ♋

Color of the day: Pink
Incense of the day: Sandalwood

Touching the Flame Spell

The element of fire represents heart, passion, energy, purification, and destruction. Its stones include garnet, carnelian, and tiger's eye; its scents include cinnamon, orange, and juniper. All the "warm colors"—red, orange, and yellow—represent fire. The best way to commune with fire, of course, is to light a fire. The best offerings are sacred woods. Many traditional woods are ideal fuel for a cookout; apple and oak in Europe, hickory and mesquite in America. Use wood chips over charcoal in a grill, or whole branches in a firepit. As you light the fire, say:

> Fire, we give you what
> You like best.
> Join us now.
> Make us blest.
>
> Fire, we share with you
> What we eat.
> Give us light.
> Give us heat.

Remember that any food that falls off the roasting stick or grill into the fire itself also belongs to the fire spirits.

Elizabeth Barrette

Notes:

August 11
Saturday

 4th ♋
☽ → ♌ 6:42 am

Color of the day: Blue
Incense of the day: Thyme

Getting Organized Spell

Organizing the home can be a very involved activity. One tip is to start small, just one drawer or closet at a time. Take a deep breath to ground and center, and begin with this chant:

> Organization is easy
> for me.
> Clarity is all I see.
> The energy comes
> times three.
> As I will it,
> So mote it be.

Now get started. There is no need to rush—take your time while doing this. Make piles of what you want to keep and what you want to give away to charity. If you feel that you're losing concentration, recite the chant. Keep going until you finish the drawer. Put away the keep pile and put the charity pile in the car. After the ritual is over, light some incense or potpourri to help clear and bless the space.

Olivia O'Meir

Notes:

August 12
Sunday

 4th ♌
New Moon 7:02 pm

Color of the day: Yellow
Incense of the day: Sage

Sunday Confidence Spell

Sunday, the day of the Sun, honors energy, success, work, and promotions. With a New Moon, it's a day to focus on a skill that will enhance our confidence, our personal strength, and how we project ourselves to others. That skill is public speaking, and it makes most people nervous. When we are asked to make a speech or a presentation either at work or at a social gathering, most of us react with dread. The thought of speaking to an audience is acknowledged as a common fear. On the day of your speech, wear something red to inspire confidence, even if it's not visible to the audience. Carry a piece of turquoise in your pocket or purse to promote verbal communication and confidence.

Emely Flak

Notes:

August 13
Monday

 1st ♌
☽ → ♍ 2:03 pm

Color of the day: Silver
Incense of the day: Sage

School Daze Spell

Whether you're school-bound, immersed in a self-study program, or have children who are students, pay heed to Saint Cassian, whose feast day is celebrated today. Cassian's students stabbed him to death with their pen nibs. Believe it or not, he is the patron saint of scholars. Line the bottom of a pottery bowl with clear quartz crystals. Hold a favorite feather with both hands. Breathing slowly over the feather, infuse it with your intentions for scholarship. See yourself, or your children, studying diligently. Your powers of focus and grasping new thoughts have strengthened. Open your eyes and watch the feather as it ruffles with your breath. Say:

> Dear Saint Cassian,
> hear my plea,
> help my mind find
> its agility.
>
> Learning is easy,
> Learning is fun,
> Without fuss or struggle,
> My schoolwork is done.

Plant the feather in your bowl of crystals and place it on your desk.

Lily Gardner

Notes:

energy. Pearls and moonstone help to balance feminine energy. Clear quartz is a good all-around attractant of universal energy.

Boudica

Notes:

August 14
Tuesday

 1st ♍

Color of the day: Gray
Incense of the day: Honeysuckle

Dog Days of Summer
Energy Booster Bags

As we come to the hottest part of the summer, it is always good to remember that plenty of liquids, especially water, will replenish our bodies and keep us balanced. Also, fresh fruits and vegetables, served cold, are refreshing, add to our personal energy, and do not weigh us down like heavy meals do. You can also carry around small spell bags to boost your energy. Use blue tourmaline (indicolite) to increase spiritual energy. Blue tiger's eye increases personal energy and strength. Rhodonite is said to restore physical

August 15
Wednesday

1st ♍

Color of the day: Topaz
Incense of the day: Honeysuckle

Computer Blessing

Take some time today to really clean your computer, monitor, and keyboard. As you clean, call to mind all the things that are made easier for you because of this computer. Be thankful that you are able to afford a computer and have the ability to use it as well as you do. Sitting at your computer desk, let go of any frustrations you have had with the computer. Allow this energy of appreciation to fill the room and connect you with your computer in an easy partnership. Say to your spirit allies and the gods you honor that you bless this computer and are thankful for its presence in your life. State that your mind is open to it, that you might more easily understand its needs and get insight into any challenges you may have in the future. Listen for any spirit messages that you might be given before going on with your day.

Kristin Madden

Notes:

August 16
Thursday

 1st ♏
☽ → ♎ 12:04 am

Color of the day: White
Incense of the day: Honeysuckle

Spell for Healing

Saint Roch, a young healer who worked tirelessly to help plague victims in the fourteenth century, is honored today. He is invoked in this spell using a crystal ball—one that is used only for healing. Pour spring water into a bowl. Hold the crystal ball in your dominant hand and say:

Oh thou stone of
Night and Right,
Let me dip thee in the
water.

In the water of
pure spring,
In the name of Saint
Roch,
In the name of the
Triple Goddess.
In the light of the
healing Sun,

Blessings on the clear
shining stone!
Blessings on the clear
pure water!
A healing of all bodily ills
On woman, man, and
beast alike!

Place the crystal ball in the water and allow the Sun to infuse it for one full day. The healing water can then be bottled and given to the sick to drink.

Lily Gardner

Notes:

August 17
Friday

 1st ♎

Color of the day: Rose
Incense of the day: Geranium

Freya's Love Spell

Thank Goddess it's Freya's day! Today call on the Norse goddess Freya for love, magic, and the development of your intuition and clairvoyant abilities. Correspondences for Freya include pink and gold candles, primroses, strawberries, the rose, and amber jewelry. This spell is perfect for drawing a little romance into your life. As always, do not target anyone specifically, or the spell will backfire. This is more than just a romance spell—it will also will bring insight and wisdom into your life. Both of these traits come in handy no matter what sort of shape your love life is in. Happy casting.

> This day is sacred to
> Freya, Norse goddess of
> love.
> Hear my request for
> magic, and answer from
> above.
>
> Send to me a lover that
> will be faithful and true.
> Bless me with insight
> and wisdom in all that
> I do.

> Ellen Dugan

Notes:

August 18
Saturday

 1st ♎
☽ → ♏ 12:13 pm

Color of the day: Indigo
Incense of the day: Sandalwood

Healing Herbal Balm

For a magical, fresh-scented balm that promotes healing in every illness from fibromyalgia to chronic fatigue syndrome, try this one. Grind together the following herbs (about 1 tsp. each): thyme, rosemary, lemon balm, mint, and cucumber zest. Hold your left arm palm up and your right palm down just over the powdered herbs. Pull healing energy from the Earth with your left hand, allowing it to completely fill your body. Visualize this energy turning a brilliant gold and sizzling with healthy energy. Push this energy out through your right hand and channel it into the herbal mixture. Add the herbs a little at a time to one stick of melted cocoa butter, stirring well after each addition. Let the balm rest until the cocoa butter base has hardened.

Tammy Sullivan

Notes:

As this new day begins,
I stand and greet the dawn,
May I help and heal others, and bring no one harm.

I rejoice in the promise of a new magical day. Bring me love, success, and health in the best possible way.

Ellen Dugan

Notes:

August 19
Sunday

 1st ♏

Color of the day: Gold
Incense of the day: Juniper

Sunrise Spell

Work this spell at sunrise and take a moment to embrace all the magic and possibilities of a brand new day. There are no other accessories needed for this spell—just yourself and the sunrise. Directions: turn and face the east. Feel the warmth and power of the Sun wash over you. Ground and center yourself, and then when you are ready repeat the charm.

August 20
Monday

 1st ♏
2nd quarter 7:54 pm

Color of the day: Ivory
Incense of the day: Clove

Sheltering Trees Ritual

After a storm, walk through the woods looking for trees that have been damaged by the winds. When you see a broken limb, look closely at the tree where the break

occurred. If you find sap running at the break, gently scrape a bit of the sap into a plain white envelope. Put a picture of yourself in the envelope. Mark the envelope with the sign of the pentacle and bury it near the base of the tree. Ask the tree to shelter you from harm and keep you safe. Promise the tree that you will care for it as well. Use a sealant on the tree at the point where the limb broke off, and add fertilizer to its roots.

Paniteowl

Notes:

August 21
Tuesday

 2nd ℠

$\mathbb{D} \rightarrow \nearrow$ 12:44 am

Color of the day: Red
Incense of the day: Frankincense

Bay Leaf Protection Amulet
A sprig of fresh bay may be hung in any room or placed under a bed for an extra boost to home protection. But a simple dried bay leaf may also be used as an amulet against all destructive forces. Leave a bay leaf on a windowsill for an hour or so early in the morning to soak up the energy of daybreak. Once you have finished the spell below, wear or carry the leaf with you throughout the day. Holding it at your forehead with both hands, say:

> Leaf of bay filled
> with light
> Of troubles and dangers,
> I have foresight.

Holding it to your heart, say:

> Shield of bay, cover me
> Safe and protected
> may I be.

Holding at the base of your spine, say:

> Tree of bay, make
> me strong
> Guide my steps that I
> will not go wrong.

Kristin Madden

Notes:

August 22
Wednesday

 2nd ♐

Color of the day: Yellow
Incense of the day: Evergreen

Celebrating Abundance

In addition to the harvest of grain which begins in the month of August, the Earth showers abundance upon us in many forms. Take time to notice the fruits of the land at this time of year: crab apples, rowan berries, blackberries, elderberries, and acorns. What fruits and other edible wild plants are available in the area where you live? There are many folk traditions associated with the gathering of "the wild bounty." In Cornwall, it was believed that blackberries should be picked before the first of October (and that blackberry stains would not disappear while the fruit was still in season). A good season of blackberries was equated with a good season of herring, an important food source in ancient times. In addition, it was considered unlucky to cut an elder tree or its blossom without first asking its permission or apologizing to the spirit of the tree.

Sharynne NicMhacha

Notes:

August 23
Thursday

 2nd ♐

☉ → ♍ 8:08 am
☽ → ♑ 11:20 am

Color of the day: Purple
Incense of the day: Cedar

Vulcanalia Ritual

Today is the Roman festival of Vulcanalia, honoring Vulcan, the Roman fire god. Working by candlelight and making offerings of fish to the god are traditional. Tonight, grill a fish dinner and put aside a portion of it for the fire god. Serve the dinner by candlelight. Bless and consecrate your stove, your microwave, your grill, your boiler, and any fireplaces in your house, honoring the god of fire. His presence eases our lives so much. Thank Vulcan for his blessings and for using fire as a comfort rather than a weapon.

Cerridwen Iris Shea

Notes:

August 24
Friday

 2nd ♑

Color of the day: Coral

Incense of the day: Musk

Finding Beauty Affirmation

In most places in the northern hemisphere at this time of year, the heat of summer is still strong. Find some time during the day or night to get outside and observe something in nature—gardens, plants, trees, or flowers. Even in the city you can usually find lovely landscaping to enjoy. Try to notice something you haven't seen before and find the beauty in it. Now look at yourself. Focus on things you like about yourself—find the beauty. Repeat this affirmation:

> help me see the beauty
> in all things,
> In people, places,
> bodies, faces.
>
> help me know the joy
> that beauty brings,
> Within us all,
> large and small.

Ember

Notes:

August 25
Saturday

 2nd ♑

☽ → ♒ 6:35 pm

Color of the day: Black

Incense of the day: Ylang-ylang

Goldenrod Spell for Wealth

In late August, goldenrod begins to star the country lanes with yellow in the Appalachian country-side where I live. When used in prosperity spells, goldenrod can attract money. The instructions for this spell are in the following verse.

> When the noble golden-
> rod raises its head,
> Cut three stems and
> bind them with golden
> thread.
>
> Do this before autumn
> leaves begin to fly,
> And hang them from a
> beam or rafter to dry.
>
> When they can be
> crumbled in your hand,
> Mix them with earth
> and sand.
>
> And one evening when
> the Moon is round,
> Sprinkle this magical
> blend upon the ground.
>
> Before the Wheel of the
> Year turns again

Abundance and wealth
will fill your hand.

James Kambos

Notes:

honeysuckle, mint, vervain; stones
like fluorite, sodalite, rutilated quartz.
Then say:

> Gold without
> Gold within
> What will be
> What has been
> Some may wait
> I create!

Glue the egg closed. Decorate the
outside with stars, spirals, or other
magical signs. Keep it in a safe place,
such as on your altar.

Elizabeth Barrette

Notes:

August 26
Sunday

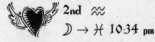

2nd ♒

Color of the day: Amber
Incense of the day: Pine

Ilmatar's Egg Spell

Today is Ilmatar's Feast Day.
According to Finnish mythology, Ilmatar is the Water Mother
who created the world. Nesting on
the waters, she laid seven eggs, six
of gold and one of iron. From these
eggs she made everything. The Finns
honor Ilmatar by feasting, dancing,
and staying up all night. What do
you create? How do you express
yourself? Celebrate your creativity by
giving it a place to live. You'll need
a hollow, resealable golden egg such
as those pantyhose come in. Fill the
egg with items corresponding to
inspiration: herbs such as cinnamon,

August 27
Monday

2nd ♒
☽ → ♓ 10:34 pm

Color of the day: Gray
Incense of the day: Basil

Saint Phanourios Cake

This special cake is baked in
honor of Saint Phanourios, a
kindly saint who helps lovers find
one another and is called upon to

locate missing objects. Before you bake the cake, say:

> Saint Phanourios, may your mother be blessed with eternal peace as you come to my aid.

The recipe:

- 1 cup sugar
- 1 cup oil
- 2 cups orange juice
- 1 tsp. baking soda
- 4 cups flour
- 3/4 cup raisins
- 3/4 cup chopped walnuts

Beat oil and sugar for 10 minutes or until creamy. In a separate bowl dissolve baking soda in orange juice (this has a tendency to foam over). Add flour, raisins, and nuts. Pour in an ungreased bundt pan or 9x13 cake pan. Bake 45 minutes at 350° F or until a toothpick inserted in the center comes out clean.

Lily Gardner

Notes:

August 28
Tuesday

 2nd ♓
Full Moon 6:35 am

Color of the day: Scarlet
Incense of the day: Myrrh

The Challenge Box

For this spell, place the following thirteen goals on slips of paper and put them in a box. They are based on the Celtic tree calendar. During ritual, take a slip from the box. Read it aloud. Allow it to inspire you and your workings for the month. Here are the goals: I honor the energy of birch for beginnings. I honor the energy of rowan for protection. I honor the energy of alder for fertility. I honor the energy of willow for the lunar cycle. I honor the energy of ash for magic. I honor the energy of hawthorn for cleansing. I honor the energy of oak for mystery. I honor the energy of holly for strength. I honor the energy of hazel for wisdom. I honor the energy of vine for celebration. I honor the energy of ivy for introspection. I honor the energy of reed for the hunt. I honor the energy of elder, which sees all.

Olivia O'Meir

Notes:

August 29
Wednesday

3rd ♓

Color of the day: White
Incense of the day: Sage

Egyptian New Year Ritual

In the ancient Egyptian calendar, today is the New Year. It was recognized as a particularly magical time when the masculine force of the Sun and the feminine force of the stars united. On this day, statues from temples and shrines were placed outside, where they could be charged with the fusion of these sacred energies. The Egyptians also believed it was the time when Sekhmet commenced her transformation back into the beautiful goddess Hathor. If there is something you wish to transform, give it careful consideration today. List only one or two things you wish to change, with an achievable time frame and steps to take. With personal development or appearance, change cannot occur overnight. Make a diary note in a few weeks' time to remind you of your goal. To seal your commitment to yourself, clean out a cupboard, rearrange furniture, or bring some fresh flowers into your room to make an immediate transformation.

Emely Flak

Notes:

August 30
Thursday

3rd ♓
☽ → ♈ 12:24 am

Color of the day: Crimson
Incense of the day: Maple

Spell to Attract Customers

Most businesses equate cash with success. To draw money to your business, make a "wash" for your floors to attract customers. Use basil with a pine-soap wash to clear negativity from the store, making it more attractive to shoppers. Add high-john-the-conqueror oil to the rinse water to attract money and encourage spending. Sprinkling cinnamon and chamomile mixture on your carpets attracts money to your store. Nightly or weekly, sprinkle some salt and pine needles on the carpet and vacuum up any negativity that may have been left in the store that day. Be sure to toss the used mixture out.

Boudica

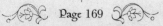

Notes:

problem, allowing it to slowly and
sweetly disappear from your life.

Gail Wood

Notes:

August 31
Friday

 3rd ♈

Color of the day: Purple
Incense of the day: Jasmine

Find the Sweetness Spell

Sometimes our lives seem to be
filled only with problems as we
move from one difficulty to another.
In focusing on troubles, we often fail
to notice that solutions and happiness reside nearby. Take one mint-
flavored LifeSavers candy and breathe
in the mint scent for clarity. Go into
a meditative state and concentrate
your vision on your problem, the
hole in your life. Slowly move your
awareness outward to the energy
around the hole, and discover the
sweetness waiting for you. Breathe
in that new awareness and knowledge into your being. While still in
meditation, put the candy into your
mouth and let it melt while you visualize the solution melting into your

September is the ninth month of the year. Its name is derived from the Latin word *septum*, which means "seventh," as it was the seventh month of the Roman calendar. Its astrological sign is Virgo, the maiden (August 23–September 23), a mutable earth sign ruled by Mercury. September is a month of fulfillment. Kitchens are busy as the garden's last produce is canned and preserved. The air is filled with the cidery tang of harvest time. Squirrels hide their nuts, and chipmunks line their nests with grain. Asters raise their purple heads, and monarch butterflies add their black-and-orange hues to autumn's palette. The sacred beverages of the season—cider and wine—echo the colors of nature now. The Fall Equinox, or Mabon, is the major holiday of September. At Mabon we celebrate the second harvest, say farewell to summer, and enter the dark season. Days grow shorter as the Great Son, Mabon, returns to Mother Earth. For the sabbat, altar decorations include pumpkins, squash, and grapes. September's Full Moon is the Harvest Moon, perhaps the most well-known of the year. It rises above the horizon and glows in solitary splendor. She is queen of the September night. The night belongs to her and her alone. Honor her by raising a glass of cider or wine, then respectfully pour it onto the earth.

September 1
Saturday

3rd ♈
☽ → ♉ 1:35 am

Color of the day: Brown
Incense of the day: Almond

Clean Slate Spell

The beginning of September turns our thoughts to fresh starts, busy school years, and heightened activity in preparation for winter. Use the attributes of the season to create your own fresh start. Purchase a small chalkboard, a few sticks of chalk, and an eraser. Bless and consecrate it in your tradition. On the board, write all the things you want to change in your life. Read the list out loud three times. Take a deep breath. Then take the eraser and wipe your slate clean. Now write an affirmation on the board. Keep it in a prominent place, speaking the affirmation at least three times a day for thirty days. Use the chalkboard to remind you that you can "wipe away" what is outmoded in your life and replace it with something positive.

Cerridwen Iris Shea

Notes:

Holiday lore: Many Greeks consider this their New Year's Day. This day marks the beginning of the sowing season, a time of promise and hope. On this day, people fashion wreaths of pomegranates, quinces, grapes, and garlic bulbs—all traditional symbols of abundance. Just before dawn on September 1, children submerge the wreaths in the ocean waters for luck. They carry seawater and pebbles home with them in small jars to serve as protection in the coming year. Tradition calls for exactly forty pebbles and water from exactly forty waves.

September 2
Sunday

3rd ♉

Color of the day: Yellow
Incense of the day: Carnation

Walk With Nature Spell

The haste of summer has passed, and with September comes a sense of peace and fulfillment. September arrives with cool misty mornings and blue morning glories blooming along the fence. In September nature begs us to walk with her—along a country road, over a ridge where you'll encounter an impatient maple tree blushed with a bit of color on a few leaves, or along a garden path where the squirrels scamper as they hide their bounty. As you walk, let your pulse slow and allow your attitude to relax. Let yourself become one with the season, and nature itself will become your altar. Along the way, respectfully gather some tokens of nature: pine cones, acorns, or a few colored leaves. When you return home, decorate with your treasures. Keep them as long as you wish, or use them later as ingredients in spell work. This is the magic of sweet September.

James Kambos

Notes:

September 3
Monday
Labor Day

 3rd ♉
☽ → ♊ 3:30 am
4th quarter 10:32 pm

Color of the day: Lavender
Incense of the day: Rose

Labor Day Spell

Kahlil Gibran said this about work: "You work that you may keep pace with the earth and the soul of the earth. For to be idle is to become a stranger unto the seasons, and to step out of life's procession, that marches in majesty and proud submission towards the infinite." Spend some time today thinking about your work. If you are dissatisfied with your current job, make a list of what you could do differently so that work would be meaningful for you. Light a green candle that you have dressed with oil of pine. Fold your work list into a tiny square and pass it through the candle smoke. Now wrap the square in a dollar bill and place it in a green bag with an agate and the Three of Pentacles tarot card. Sleep with this bag under your pillow for thirteen nights.

Lily Gardner

Notes:

September 4
Tuesday

 4th ♊

Color of the day: Red
Incense of the day: Rose

Energy Restoring Bath

The kids are back to school, and you are drained from summer activities and pre-school preparation. To restore personal energy, try relaxing in a tub of hot water and adding lavender and peppermint to the bath. Lily of the valley restores inner peace. Basil oil refreshes. Adding salts to the bath will allow you to ground negativity and start fresh. Do a meditation, allowing tiredness to wash off you in the shower and go down the drain. See the water from the shower head as revitalizing and washing new energy over you. Follow up with a soaping of your favorite energizing fragrances.

Boudica

Notes:

September 5
Wednesday

4th ♊
☽ → ♋ 7:08 am

Color of the day: Topaz
Incense of the day: Musk

Slow Down and See the Colors Spell

In early September, our lives become rushed while the colors of fall begin to make their very brief appearance. If we are not careful, we will miss them. To slow down and notice them, create a small ritual. In a saucepan, simmer together one quart apple cider or juice (sacred connection to the Goddess) with two cinnamon sticks (spiritual connection) and eight cloves (love and purity), three-quarters of a cup of lemon juice (for friendship with nature), and one cup firmly packed brown sugar (for sweetness). After 20 minutes, pour yourself a generous portion and go outside and watch the leaves. Sip slowly and savor each smell and taste. Yellow leaves remind us of joy, creativity, and communication with others. Orange reminds us of the sensuality all around us, and golden leaves remind us of prosperity and our connection with the dying of the Earth. Green leaves remind us of the promise of renewal and things yet to come.

Gail Wood

Notes:

Notes:

September 6
Thursday

 4th ☌

Color of the day: Green
Incense of the day: Pine

Quick Cash Spell

Are you a little short on cash? Then banish those money woes with this little spell. This would be a good spell to use before selling items online or holding a yard sale. You will need play cash (like Monopoly money), a green candle, and some rosemary essential oil. Anoint the candle with the oil, thinking of your bills marked "paid" and your pantry full. Place the play cash under the candle and light it. Hold your hands on either side of the candle and infuse it with your will. Visualize your wallet full of money, your bank account well in the black, and your needs generally met. Let the candle burn for the hour and it is done.

Laurel Reufner

September 7
Friday

 4th ☌

☽ → ♌ 12:59 pm

Color of the day: White
Incense of the day: Chrysanthemum

Cornwall Folk Charms

Before winter sets in, herbalists and wise-women spent time in nature collecting the plants and herbs they needed for effecting cures during the winter season. In Cornwall, plants such as bramble (blackberry), ivy, rowan, chamomile, dock, and club moss were used in healing charms. In Cornish folk tradition, it was believed that charmers could not accept money and that the patient must not say "thank you." Sometimes powerful charmers were able to effect cures without seeing the patient in person (this was also true in Scotland and Ireland). In this case, the charmer might work with a piece of the patient's clothing, breathing their power into and reciting charms over the item. Secrets for charming were believed to only be handed down to someone of the opposite sex.

Sharynne NicMhacha

Notes:

sharp; prune correctly, leaving a small smooth cut; and paint the raw wood with horticultural sealant if you wish. Over the cut ends, trace the rune Ehwaz (which looks like a line with a hook at top and bottom). Ehwaz means "yew tree" and it grants protection, defense, strength, and endurance.

Elizabeth Barrette

Notes:

September 8
Saturday

4th ♌

Color of the day: Gray
Incense of the day: Nutmeg

Autumn Rune Spell

Autumn is an excellent time for pruning of all kinds. As winter approaches, we get rid of things we don't need. We rake leaves to compost. We harvest the last of summer's herbs and dig up the ragged annuals, leaving the garden ready to rest. We trim awkward branches from the trees. Though often necessary, pruning branches can leave a tree vulnerable to invasion from insects or disease. To prevent this, make sure your shears are clean and

September 9
Sunday

4th ♌
☽ → ♏ 9:10 pm

Color of the day: Orange
Incense of the day: Jasmine

Sunny Day Healing Spell

Here is a sunny, healing, and successful spell for a Sunday. You will need a small yellow votive candle, a votive cup, and a safe place to let the candle burn out. Take a straight pin or nail and carve a simple Sun design on the side of the candle. Now secure the candle back in its holder. Light it and visualize success, health, and wealth coming to you in the best, most productive way. Now repeat the spell three times. When finished, allow the candle to burn out on its own.

> On this magical day of
> the bright golden Sun,
> Grant me success and
> wealth, so long as it
> harms none.
>
> Now make me happy,
> wealthy, healthy,
> and wise,
> As the golden Sun lights
> up today's blue skies.

Ellen Dugan

Notes:

September 10
Monday

 4th ♏

Color of the day: White
Incense of the day: Jasmine

Sew Be Me Spell

Sometimes we are our own worst enemies. Our images of self are so low that we sabotage our own successes by listening to that vicious inner voice that tells us bad things about ourselves. When we believe these internal lies directed at us, we clothe ourselves in the garments of failure. This simple poppet spell can be hand sewn with a needle and thread, or you can use a sewing machine, which was patented on this day in 1846. On a plain piece of fabric that generally matches your skin tone, draw a simple outline of a person, marking in some way your attributes according to gender and body type. Cut out two of these outlines. Go into a meditative state with these two fabric pieces in your hand. Envision what you are when you do not listen to this negative voice. Envision yourself clothed in talent, success, pride, beauty, and power. Still in meditation, open your eyes and, using various pens, crayons, and other implements, write or draw symbols and adjectives that describe you as you envisioned. Keeping your vision in mind, chant, "Sew be me" as you sew those two pieces of fabric together with the drawn sides facing inward, leaving an open space at the head. Stuff the poppet with quilt batting or cotton balls. Be sure to include any other herbs, small gemstones, or beads that enhance your inner strength. Finish off the poppet and draw the facial features. Clothe the poppet in fabric and decorate it beautifully. Keep the doll in a safe place, visiting it often, until your role as your own worst enemy disappears. Then lovingly take the doll apart and bury the parts in Mother Earth, thanking her for your strength and wisdom.

Gail Wood

Notes:

September 11
Tuesday

4th ♏
New Moon 8:44 am

Color of the day: Maroon
Incense of the day: Daffodil

Eclipsing Old Habits Spell

A solar eclipse occurs as the Sun casts the Moon's shadow across the Earth. It unites the powers of Sun and Moon, light and darkness, logic and intuition. It is "a day without a night, a night without a day," magically suspended from normal routines: a cosmic exception that proves the rule of Sun and Moon. An eclipse is a perfect time for changing patterns. Use its power to break curses, bad habits, and so forth. Choose a small item representing what you want to dispel. At the time of the eclipse, take the item far from your home. Hold it and concentrate on all that binds and limits you, symbolized by this object. Then say:

> Eclipse, break
> through the past
> Smashing all
> that held me fast.
>
> Shadow come,
> shadow go,
> Take this nasty
> thing I throw.

Throw the item as far away from you as possible. Quickly bury it where it falls, then say:

> Hide it far, far away
> Lost between the night
> and day.
> Leave it there, let it be,
> Never more to
> trouble me!

Cover the site with fallen leaves or grass to obscure it. Then walk away without looking back.

Elizabeth Barrette

Notes:

Unwanted presence
now be gone,
Trouble me no more.

I banish this
unwelcome force,
Trouble me no more.

Cause me no more pain,
Go back from where
you came,

Trouble me no more.

Ember

Notes:

September 12
Wednesday

 1st ♍
☽ → ♎ 7:31 am

Color of the day: Yellow
Incense of the day: Neroli

Trouble Me No More Spell

Harness the power of Mercury, the winged messenger, to carry away an unwanted presence. Remember to act instead of reacting to a situation, and don't let yourself feel out of control or controlled by others. Use this spell to correct an unpleasant situation. Use incense of frankincense, dragon's blood, and sage to smudge the area, and sprinkle a few drops of cedar oil on the ground or floor, or draw a pentacle or other protective symbol with the oil. Visualize negative energy being dispersed into harmless neutral energy. Imagine a shield surrounding you.

September 13
Thursday

Rosh hashanah – Ramadan begins

 1st ♎

Color of the day: Turquoise
Incense of the day: Rose

The Night Prayer

During the holy month of Ramadan, Muslims recite the *Taraweeh* prayer at night. This is a longer prayer than most daily prayers and some Muslims have been known to spend all night in prayer. In honor of this unique month-long holy period, non-Muslims may want to offer a nightly prayer each evening for a week or a month. Just before bed, stand outside or by a window and begin with a review of your day. Let go of any regrets or frustrations and end by giving thanks for even the smallest blessings. Give thanks for the Moon and stars and the fact that you are able to appreciate the wonders of the night. With each step on your way to bed, offer a blessing for yourself, someone you know, or the world. As you lie down to sleep, ask for beautiful dreams to fill your night.

Kristin Madden

Notes:

September 14
Friday

1st ♎
☽ → ♏ 7:37 pm

Color of the day: Rose
Incense of the day: Evergreen

Back to School Spell

Cut a length of holly approximately 8 inches long. Wrap the stem with a copper wire, leaving the leaves free of the wire. Tie a red ribbon to the wrapped stem and hang the holly in whatever room homework is done. As you hang the talisman, remember that the time of the Holly King is one of rest, reflection, and learning. Say these words:

> Now it's time for
> back to school,
> this child of mine
> will be no fool.

(Or, if you're the one going back to school: "My mother hasn't raised a fool.")

> May knowledge be
> the golden key.
> As I will, so mote it be!

Before a test, or if you're struggling with a particularly difficult subject, break off one of the holly leaves and put it in the book to help you concentrate.

Paniteowl

 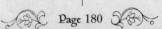

Notes:

bath with your favorite oil. Imagine the healing properties of water relaxing and energizing you. After your bath, adorn your body in a tropical scented lotion such as coconut, banana, or papaya, and honor your sacred feminine energy.

Emely Flak

Notes:

September 15
Saturday

 1st ♏

Color of the day: Blue
Incense of the day: Ginger

hawaiian Ritual Bath

In Hawaii, during the month of September, the Aloha festival is celebrated. Although this festival commenced in the 1940s to celebrate the diversity of cultures that exist in Hawaii, the choice of autumn for this event has Pagan origins. In ancient Hawaii, it was the time of Makahiki, which is the period following the harvest. This makes it a good time to honor a Hawaiian deity. Hina, one of the oldest Hawaiian goddesses, is also known throughout the Pacific as Sina or Ina. Her name is derived from the word *wahine*, which means "woman," so it's no surprise that she represents feminine energy, the Moon, and the ocean. To connect with Hina today, take a luxurious

Holiday Lore: Keirou no Hi, or "Respect for the Aged Day," has been a national holiday in Japan since 1966. On this day, the Japanese show respect to elderly citizens, celebrate their longevity, and pray for their health. Although there are no traditional customs specifically associated with this day, cultural programs are usually held in various communities. School children draw pictures or make handicraft gifts for their grandparents and elderly family friends or neighbors. Some groups visit retirement or nursing homes to present gifts to residents.

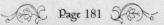

September 16
Sunday

 1st ♏

Color of the day: Gold
Incense of the day: Violet

Saint Ninian's Day Passion Spell

Ninian's plant is the herb southernwood. Used as an aphrodisiac, southernwood's folk name is "Lad's Love." To rekindle passion in your relationship, cast this knotting spell. Begin by cutting a length of red cord equal to your height. Insert a sprig of southernwood in each of your nine knots while you chant the knotting spell:

> Knot of one,
> the spell's begun.
>
> Knot of two,
> it cometh true.
>
> Knot of three,
> so shall it be.
>
> Knot of four,
> the open door.
>
> Knot of five,
> the spell's alive.
>
> Knot of six,
> the spell is fixed.
>
> Knot of seven,
> the gates of heaven.

> Knot of eight,
> the hand of fate.
>
> Knot of nine,
> the spell is mine.

Fasten the ends of the cord so that it forms a circle and place it under your bed.

Lily Gardner

Notes:

September 17
Monday

 1st ♏
☽ → ♐ 8:21 am

Color of the day: Silver
Incense of the day: Poplar

Banishing Illness Ritual

Banishing spells can be useful in healing work. To create an effective banishing spell, you really need one thing: a clear, well-chosen, long-term goal. Before this spell, take time to meditate seriously on your goal. Where and what do you want to heal? Try to focus on the core illness, not just the symptoms. Throughout this simple ritual, focus on this goal. Find a comfortable and safe place. Light a green candle and some sage incense. Now say:

> Brighid, blessed goddess of healing arts, hear my prayers. Please be here with me tonight. I ask for your help in banishing this illness, as one of your children. Wash away the illness with your sacred waters.
>
> Shining goddess, fill me with power, strength, and bravery.

Olivia O'Meir

Notes:

pearance of our laptops and notebooks? Since these computers are meant to be portable, they deserve a little extra protection. For this charm, you will need a luggage tag. You will also need a red candle, some paper, and a red pen. Find a quiet place at night, light the candle, and upon the paper write,

> May whoever harms me cease ever to have a moment's peace. May this computer be protected by the very gods themselves.

Slip the paper into the back of the luggage tag, fill in your information on the front, and let it rest near the candle until the candle has burnt down completely.

Laurel Reufner

Notes:

September 18
Tuesday

1st ♍ ♐

Color of the day: White
Incense of the day: Peony

Laptop Protection Spell

How many of us would be more than a little lost at the disap-

September 19
Wednesday

1st ♐

2nd quarter 12:48 pm

☽ → ♑ 7:51 pm

Color of the day: Topaz
Incense of the day: Pine

Swift Mercury Spell

Wednesdays are Mercury days. This day of the week belongs to the winged-footed god Mercury. This makes today a perfect day for casting spells for cunning, speed, and communication. Do you feel like nothing is moving forward in your life? Are you stuck in a rut and want to shake things up? Call on Mercury for assistance—he'll bring change and movement blazing into your life. But remember, Mercury is a trickster. So this spell closes with a tag line, ensuring that the magic unfolds in the best possible way.

> Wednesdays are for
> Mercury, that quick
> and nimble god,
>
> A clever and canny soul,
> on winged feet
> he does trod.
>
> I'm stuck in a rut,
> so help me to break
> gently free,

With no trouble or harm,
as I will so mote it be.

Ellen Dugan

Notes:

September 20
Thursday

2nd ♑

Color of the day: Purple
Incense of the day: Coriander

Wash Away the Day Spell

It's almost the equinox, when night and day are in balance, making it a good time to evaluate aspects of our lives that also require balance. In the business of our daily lives, we work long hours and often forget to unwind. After a day at work or school that demands a great deal of your time and energy, take a shower and imagine the stress of the day washing down the drain. Change into clothing that is comfortable. When you are in the shower, watch the water wash away and say:

> Wash away the day
> and pain

And all problems
down the drain.

As they disappear
I am now free
To nurture just me!

This short ritual affirms the separation between your working day and your sacred time for yourself. Any ongoing issues will still be at work or school tomorrow, whether you worry or not, so you may as well not! While you are home, free yourself from the burden of concern and enjoy balance in your life.

Emely Flak

Notes:

a pink candle and burn a pleasing incense. Write a list of people you deal with on a regular basis: friends, family, co-workers, the guy at the deli, the girl who sells you the lottery tickets. Next to each name write your favorite thing about the person. An important part of harvest is to share and celebrate. Take a stack of postcards. Let each person on the list know what it is you like best about him or her. Before you mail the cards, kiss each one and say, "Sent with love."

Cerridwen Iris Shea

Notes:

September 21
Friday

 2nd ♑

Color of the day: Pink
Incense of the day: Dill

Loving harvest Spell

Today is a special day. With the Fall Equinox—the middle harvest festival—so close, and today being Friday, the day of Venus, it's time for a Loving Harvest. Light

September 22
Saturday
Yom Kippur

 2nd ♑
☽ → ♒ 4:18 am

Color of the day: Indigo
Incense of the day: Rose

Divination Tool Blessing

To cleanse and recharge your divination tools, try the following simple spell. In your mortar,

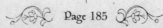

grind together orange zest, orris root, salt, hibiscus petals, and dandelion leaves. As you grind, concentrate on blessing the tool. Once the herbs are ground to a powder, sprinkle them over the tool and wrap it in a cloth of white linen. Place the bundle under a large, clear quartz crystal. Say,

> Blessed be this tool, for
> it shows me a new view.
> Blessed be this tool,
> for the Lord and Lady
> communicate with me
> through it. Blessed be
> this tool, for it works
> with me in harmony.

Allow the tool to sit for a while and absorb the blessings. Unwrap and kiss the deck before shuffling. This spell can be performed at any time to keep your tool fresh and clean while allowing it to maintain its bond with you.

Tammy Sullivan

Notes:

September 23
Sunday
Mabon – Fall Equinox

 2nd ≈

☉ → ♎ 5:51 am

Color of the day: Amber
Incense of the day: Cedar

Mabon Meditation

The Autumnal Equinox is a time of balance between light and dark, and many Pagans utilize this powerful turning point by doing magical work for balancing the energies in their life. The modern Neopagan name for this holiday is "Mabon." It is a bit mysterious why early twentieth-century occultists chose this name for the holiday, as this is a Middle Welsh word which means "Divine Son." Mabon is a somewhat shadowy figure who is mentioned only briefly in several medieval Welsh myths. However, his name may reflect an earlier British god, Maponus, who was widely worshipped in Britain and Gaul. One of his attributes was hunting, and in a later Welsh tale, Mabon assisted with the sacred boar hunt that takes place before Samhain. Meditate on the "Divine Son" and his ancient role in the ritual hunts that took place in autumn.

Sharynne NicMhacha

Notes:

By the power of herb
from antiquity,
My body is rested, my
mind is free.

Paniteowl

Notes:

September 24
Monday

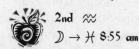

2nd ≈
☽ → ♓ 8:55 am

Color of the day: Ivory
Incense of the day: Cinnamon

Lavender Anxiety Spell

Lavender is an age-old remedy for stress. We're fortunate today that we can get bath oils, shower gels, body lotions, and candles with lavender as part of the recipe. When you're feeling especially stressed, take advantage of those modern preparations and take a soothing bath or lukewarm shower using the lavender preparations. Light a lavender-scented candle and put a lavender sachet inside your pillowcase. Breathe deeply as you rub lavender-scented skin softener over your body. Let the magic of lavender soothe your mind as well as your body. As you lie down to sleep, breathe deeply, in and out, and envision the lavender calming your body and mind.

September 25
Tuesday

2nd ♓

Color of the day: Gray
Incense of the day: Lavender

Home Energy Spell

To balance the energies within your home, take three red apples and cut them in half horizontally, so the pentagram of the seeds shows. Place an apple half at each of the cardinal points in your home, along with a white candle. A fifth apple goes near the home's center, along with another white candle. Beginning in the east, light each candle. Envision a set of scales in perfect balance and glowing with a blue-white light. Light the fifth candle and feel the calmness of balance settling over you and your home. Allow the candles to burn down completely and it is done. Dispose of the apples outside if at all possible.

Laurel Reufner

Notes:

September 26
Wednesday

2nd ♓

☽ → ♈ 10:22 am

Full Moon 3:45 pm

Color of the day: Yellow
Incense of the day: Juniper

harvest Full Moon Ritual

have at hand those things that remind you of this time of year—harvest goods of fresh ears of corn, pumpkin pie, and apples or apple cider. These will be your "cakes and ale." Gather things that remind you of your accomplishments this year: business items, papers from a new job, something you have made. Add pictures of your family and friends. All items should be associated with personal success. Find a place where your feet touch ground, the sky is open, and you can see the

Moon. Otherwise, choose a comfortable space where you can close your eyes and "feel" the ground and "see" the Moon. Surround yourself with sacred space and call upon your deities to join you. Now look around at all the things you have gathered. This is your harvest: successes that have grown from your creative mind or personal skills. Give thanks to your deities for your harvest this year. Eat the foods that you brought into the circle. Finally, clear out your sacred space. And remember to take leftovers outside to share with the spirits of the harvest.

Boudica

Notes:

September 27
Thursday
Sukkot begins

3rd ♈

Color of the day: White
Incense of the day: Rose

healing After a Storm

thursday is named for Thor, Germanic thunder god, similar to the Roman sky god Jupiter.

Thor's hammer is a symbol for the creative and destructive powers of nature. Think of storms in your life as having this same destructive yet creative power. Renewal follows the storm, even when there is destruction. Meditate on this cycle when you need to find balance and seek solace after a storm in your life. Use the hammer as a symbol if you wish. Visualize a storm—high winds, rain, thunder, lightning, and hail—but see it moving away from you. Note that where lightning has caused a fire; that same fire has caused dormant seeds to sprout. Imagine your personal storm that way. See the rain washing away the old and the new seeds sprouting, as in the natural world.

Ember

Notes:

September 28
Friday

 3rd ♈
☽ → ♉ 10:17 am

Color of the day: Coral
Incense of the day: Carnation

Mother Mawu Spell

This ritual calls to the African goddess Mawu from the Dahomey tribe. Mawu is a creator and Moon goddess whose blessings include inspiration and fertility. She is a goddess of creativity and birth.

> Mother Mawu, creatrix of the world, come to me riding the elephant's back and following the bright Moon. Inspire me, bless my new projects, and bless me with abundance. Mother Mawu, I call to you. Thank you for your presence.

Light a candle and chant to raise energy. Focus on your new beginnings and cup your hands. See your goal inside your hands. Chant:

> Mother Mawu, as I begin, favor my goals within.

Once the energy has peaked, take the energy and send it through your hands to your goal.

Olivia O'Meir

Notes:

September 29
Saturday

3rd ♉
Color of the day: Black
Incense of the day: Carnation

Michaelmas

On Michaelmas, the feast of Saint Michael is observed in the churches of the West. It is a day to dine on goose for good luck, and in some European nations it's a time to pay rents and take care of business. In some areas of southern Europe he is invoked when someone wishes to break the curse of the evil eye. He is the Christianized aspect of the god Mars. And he also resembles the Lord of the Wild Hunt, the god force that leads the spirits from the otherworld as they ride horseback across the night skies of autumn and winter. Like the leader of the Wild Hunt, he is not only both warrior and protector, he also receives the souls of the dead. Water and high places such as hills are sacred to Saint Michael. If you need Saint Michael's aid, it is traditionally done by saying his name out loud three times. Then proceed to ask him for help concerning your specific need.

James Kambos

Notes:

September 30
Sunday

3rd ♉
☽ → ♊ 10:34 am

Color of the day: Yellow
Incense of the day: Patchouli

Curb Unhealthy Habits Spell

This simple spell can help when we are challenged with monumental tasks such as quitting smoking or following super-strict dietary guidelines. Take an egg and paint it black. Gently drill a small hole in each end with your athame. Blow out the contents, leaving only the empty shell. Write the challenge on a small slip of paper and slip it into the shell. Be specific: if the actual challenge is cigarette cravings, write exactly that. Throughout the day, channel the energy from cravings into the shell with your third eye. At the end of the day, take the shell and place it on a sturdy surface and say,

> With this blow,
> the cravings go.
> So mote it be!

Smash the shell with a hammer or other heavy object.

Tammy Sullivan

Notes:

October is the tenth month of the year, its name derived from the Latin word meaning "eight," as it was the eighth month of the Roman calendar. Its astrological sign is Libra, the scales (September 23–October 23), a cardinal air sign ruled by Venus. In October we enter the glorious late afternoon of the year. Bittersweet berries turn brilliant orange, and the woodland blazes with vibrant colors reminscent of a Persian carpet. As October passes, the door to the otherworld opens wider. We become more receptive to spiritual energies and feel drawn to bond with our ancestors. The main holiday of October, and one of the most magical nights of the year, is Samhain, or Halloween. This is a traditional time to honor our ancestors. Many seasonal decorations can help do this. The jack-o'-lantern illuminates a path so the spirits of our ancestors can find their way. Apples are used to feed the dead, so leave an apple near your door or on a plate at your table. The name of October's Full Moon, the Blood Moon, comes from this urge to connect with ancestors. When the Blood Moon rises, it smolders like an ember in the autumn sky. She is a beacon for spiritual energy. Thank her by leaving an apple beneath a tree, or by burning some dried wormwood in a dish and meditating on your deceased loved ones.

October 1
Monday

 3rd ♊

Color of the day: Gray
Incense of the day: Sage

Bringing the Money In Spell

For this spell, light some green and gold candles anointed with cinnamon oil. Also, burn some cinnamon, frankincense, and myrrh incense on charcoal. Take five shiny new pennies and hold them in your dominant hand and chant:

> When I give away these
> pennies I see, more
> money will come to me.
> So mote it be.

Visualize money being given to you in many forms, like cash, checks, or gifts. When the spell is finished, give the pennies away by buying things, making change, or donating to charity. This simple money spell requires faith that the universe will provide. There also must be a belief in the natural give and take of prosperity: to receive, you must give; to give, you must receive.

Olivia O'Meir

Notes:

Holiday lore: According to Shinto belief, during the month of October the gods gather to hold their annual convention. All of the *kami* converge on the great temple of Isumo in western Honshu, and there they relax, compare notes on crucial god business, and make decisions about humankind. At the end of this month, all over Japan, people make visits to their local Shinto shrines to welcome the regular resident gods back home. But until then, all through the month, the gods are missing—as a Japanese poet once wrote:

> The god is absent;
> the dead leaves are
> piling up,
> and all is deserted.

October 2
Tuesday

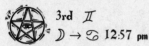

3rd ♊
☽ → ♋ 12:57 pm

Color of the day: Red
Incense of the day: Maple

Guiding Spirits Day

This is the day when Pagans give thanks to their spirit guides for their protection and counsel. Light a purple candle. Burn a mixture of bay, lemongrass, and mugwort. Center and meditate for at least twenty minutes, reviewing the past year. Pay attention in your review to the times when you heeded an inner voice, and the way that affected your choices. Start a new practice of journaling each time you act on your inner voice. Also, try journaling every time you experience synchronicity in your life. This serves to strengthen the connection between you and your guides. Give thanks to your guides for their guardianship. Do you have questions for them? See if you can contact them through scrying, a tarot reading, or through the Ouija board.

Lily Gardner

Notes:

October 3
Wednesday

Sukkot ends

3rd ♋
4th quarter 6:06 am

Color of the day: Brown
Incense of the day: Rose

Magical Creature Alignment

There are a myriad of magical creatures with which we can work. In order to find your best match, take the time and do some research. On a deck of blank index cards, put the name, drawing, or other depiction of each animal on a separate card. Ground and center.
Say:

> Swing and sway,
> find a way,
> guide me to
> my ally on this day.

Use your pendulum over each card to find out which one is your best ally for the next cycle of your life.
Start working with your creature, getting to know it and forming a magical partnership.

Cerridwen Iris Shea

Notes:

October 4
Thursday

 4th ♋

☽ → ♌ 6:27 pm

Color of the day: Turquoise
Incense of the day: Eucalyptus

Jejunium Cereris

Ceres is the mother goddess of all growing things and of creativity. As the goddess of living beings, Ceres governs over decline and death—the inevitable fate of the living. In ancient Rome, Pagans honored Ceres today in a day of fasting. Mystics have often used fasting to signal their physical bodies that change is coming. Think of fasting not as a deprivation but as an opportunity to observe the holes in our lives we are filling with food, sex, smoking, compulsive shopping, or television. Fasting is a way to regain self-control, thereby empowering us. Whatever you choose to fast from today, make it something that is meaningful enough that you will feel the sense of strength from having fasted from it. At day's close, burn an orange candle. Ask Ceres to guide you into leading a more creative life.

Lily Gardner

Notes:

October 5
Friday

 4th ♌

Color of the day: White
Incense of the day: Geranium

Mirror of My Smile Spell

Fridays contain the magic of love, beauty, and relationships, and nothing shows more beauty and brings more joy than a smiling face. Finding beauty in our own image is often very difficult. Spend some time pampering yourself with pleasant lotions and powders. Wash your face with rose soap for beauty. Bring together a mirror, lavender incense, and a violet candle. In a semi-dark room breathe in the beauty of the scent and the candle's glow. Look at your reflection in the mirror. Begin by making ugly faces and grimaces. Take a deep breath and close your eyes. Whisper three times, "Thou art Goddess and thou art God." Breathe in that magical statement. Smile and open your eyes, looking straight into the reflection in the mirror. See how beautiful you are!

Gail Wood

Notes:

October 6
Saturday

 4th ♌

Color of the day: Black
Incense of the day: Almond

harvest Knotwork

Throughout the month of October, farmers worked hard to bring in the grain harvest during the good weather (and before the end of the year at Samhain). In Ireland, as part of the harvest celebration, small ornamental twists or knots of braided straw were created and worn as a sign that the harvest was completed. These were made throughout the harvest season, and were also worn at the "Harvest Home" supper. Women wore elaborately created knots with the grain ears still attached, and men wore simpler knots without the ears. Patterns for harvest knot-making are easy to find online. After soaking the straw, think about what prayers or magical work you would like to weave into the harvest-knot. Repeat your charm or prayer as you make your magical autumn weaving.

Sharynne NicMhacha

Notes:

October 7
Sunday

 4th ♌

☽ → ♍ 3:03 am

Color of the day: Orange
Incense of the day: Lilac

Ma'at's Justice Spell

Today is the feast day of Ma'at, Egyptian goddess of justice and fairness, whose symbol is an ostrich feather. In mythology, Ma'at's feather was used to weigh against mortal hearts in the Hall of Justice to determine their fate in the afterlife. Is there an issue in your life at the moment that can benefit from the attention of Ma'at, requiring more equity? For this spell you will need a feather and a blue candle. On the candle, engrave the symbol of a feather and the name of Ma'at. If you have any items that relate to the injustice, such as a letter, place them on your altar. Light the candle and say:

> There is a situation that seems unfair,
>
> I look for an outcome that harms none.
>
> Ma'at, you have a right to effect what you deem is fair
>
> To ensure that order and justice are done.

Emely Flak

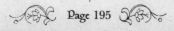

Notes:

Now don't push your luck on this one! Stop at the next service station and put air in your tires!

Paniteowl

Notes:

October 8
Monday
Columbus Day (observed)

 4th ♏

Color of the day: Lavender
Incense of the day: Chrysanthemum

Travel in Safety Spell

At the time Columbus traveled, there were many spells used by sailors and their families to ensure a safe voyage. Today, we travel every day by car or by public transportation, and there are a variety of spells we may use to ensure our safe arrival home. Here's one a friend uses quite often and effectively. As soon as you hear your tires screeching as you make a turn, ask in a very loud voice:

> Lord Vulcan, full of
> power and fire,
> grant me now
> my one desire:
> that I get home on this
> flat tire.

October 9
Tuesday

 4th ♏
☽ → ♎ 1:57 pm

Color of the day: White
Incense of the day: Chrysanthemum

Pet Protection Spell

It is common to go out of town or on vacation and leave the family pet at home. We see to their food, water, and shelter needs, but often we forget to add any magical protection to keep them safe. Long ago, people hung holey stones near where the pet slept. Today, our pets have collars and we can sew the stones directly onto it. Use red thread for added power and visualize the collar wrapping your pet in a protective bubble while you sew. When

placing the collar on the pet, affirm:

> (Your pet's name) is
> under the protection of
> the Lord and Lady.
> She is safe. She is safe.
> She is safe.
> It is so!

Tammy Sullivan

Notes:

October 10
Wednesday

4th ♎

Color of the day: Topaz
Incense of the day: Evergreen

Autumn Garden Blessing

The autumn months are the perfect time to add to your gardens. Take a moment and bless your crocus, tulip, hyacinth, and daffodil bulbs as you tuck them in the garden this autumn. A general rule of thumb is to plant the bulb two to three times deeper than the length of the bulb itself, and if you can't distinguish between top and bottom, just plant the bulb on its side: the shoots will instinctively grow to the sun. Dig your holes and set the bulbs. As you go to cover them back up, tap the soil three times with your dominant hand and repeat this charm.

> Planted deep in autumn,
> to shoot forth in spring,
>
> Beauty, joy, and
> enchantment these bulbs
> will bring.
>
> Now sleep the winter
> away and store your
> energy well,
>
> Next spring you'll grow
> both tall and true, all
> from this autumn spell.

Ellen Dugan

Notes:

 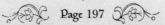

October 11
Thursday

 4th ♎
New Moon 1:01 am

Color of the day: Green
Incense of the day: Cedar

The Money Bottle

To make a money-spell bottle, place a piece each of jade, tiger's eye, and aventurine into a small corked bottle. Add a pinch of salt, tea, and basil. Toss in five cloves. Fill the bottle almost full of extra virgin olive oil. Cork the bottle tightly. Light a green candle and carefully drip the melting wax over the top of the bottle to seal it. Let it sit on a windowsill in the now-increasing moonlight for the next week, spending a moment now and then looking at the bottle and its contents and imagining your money problems disappearing. Put the bottle in a safe place out of sight.

Laurel Reufner

Notes:

October 12
Friday

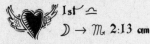 1st ♎
☽ → ♏ 2:13 am

Color of the day: Rose
Incense of the day: Cedar

Runic Friendship Spell

Carve the rune *wunjo* or *wynn* into a lemon. The rune brings harmony and fellowship, among other things. Holding the lemon up as an offering to your spirit allies, chant the rune's name three times. Then state your intent to attract and appreciate healthy relationships with true friends.

> hail to the gods and
> the wights
>
> hail to the ancestors and
> loved ones
>
> hail to friendship and
> honor
>
> May I be create deep
> and abiding friendships
> And may I be worthy of
> such blessings

As you squeeze the juice into a glass of water, chant the rune's name three more times. Pour some of your water out onto the earth in honor of the old gods, and drink the rest.

Kristin Madden

Notes:

food bank. In some small way it may help us appreciate the Islamic tradition of fasting, and at the same time we have a chance to help others.

James Kambos

Notes:

October 13
Saturday

Ramadan ends

 1st ♏

Color of the day: Gray
Incense of the day: Cedar

Breaking the Fast

The Islamic month of Ramadan, a month of strict fasting, ends today. Muslims observe this by enjoying a three-day celebration known as Festival of the Breaking of the Fast. Visiting and exchanging small gifts are common activities today, and families prepare favorite foods. Since breaking the fast is a major theme today, people of all faiths can learn something from this Islamic experience. To begin, prepare or purchase one of your favorite foods, but don't eat it. Instead, share it with friends or an elderly person who finds it hard to cook. You may also purchase food and donate it to a

October 14
Sunday

 1st ♏
☽ → ♐ 2:58 pm

Color of the day: Yellow
Incense of the day: Juniper

Wish Upon the Sun

Almost everyone knows the nursery rhyme "Star Light, Star Bright" and the tradition of wishing on a star. But sometimes we forget the stars are shining all the time, all day long. Our nearest star, the Sun, is so close and shines so brightly that we can't see them. So, the tradition of wishing on a star can be done anytime—especially if you wish upon the Sun. Use this day to wish on the Sun and all the surrounding stars for

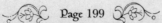

your heart's desire. But remember—
be careful what you wish for! Write
your wish on yellow paper and decorate it with symbols of the Sun and
stars. Think back to your childhood
and have fun! Use a gold marker or
stickers. Then read your wish out
loud beneath the sunlight.

Ember

Notes:

October 15
Monday

 1st ♐

Color of the day: White
Incense of the day: Basil

Winter's Day Spell
The Romans celebrated today
as Winter's Day. All summer
activities ended on this day as the
Romans prepared for winter. Light
a white candle and burn a stick of
lavender incense. Spend as much of
the day as possible cleaning closets,
storing summer clothes, stacking
firewood—whatever tasks you under-
take to ready yourself for the winter

season. Perform these tasks with
mindfulness and joy. To celebrate the
coming of winter, build a fire tonight.
Looking into the flames, say:

> Winter's day,
> Winter's night,
> Blazing fire,
> shining bright,
> Give me now
> the second sight.

Images may appear within the flames
or in the burning embers beneath
them. Reflect on how these images
may guide you in your efforts this
season.

Lily Gardner

Notes:

October 16
Tuesday

 1st ♐

Color of the day: Black
Incense of the day: Frankincense

Making a Water Altar
The element of water relates to
the soul, emotions, intuition,
cleansing, tides, and cycles. The

scents of water include gardenia, jasmine, rose, and sandalwood; its stones include aquamarine, chrysocolla, lapis lazuli, and moonstone. Its main color is blue, with secondary associations to limpid shades of lavender and green, and gray and white. Even if you have very little space, you can enjoy a water altar. For this, you need a large, clear glass vase. Put some blue marbles in the bottom and a mesh tray in the neck to hold plant cuttings which will root. (Some people like to add a single fish.) Consecrate it with these words:

> Sacred water in a vase
> Spread your blessings
> through this place
> Wash away despair
> and strife
> Fill the space with
> hope and life.

Keep your water altar in bright, indirect sunlight and repeat the rhyme whenever you add or change water.

Elizabeth Barrette

Notes:

October 17
Wednesday

 1st ♐
☽ → ♑ 3:03 am

Color of the day: Brown
Incense of the day: Juniper

Guardian Spirit Spell

It is said we all have a guardian spirit. All we need to do is focus our attention on communicating with it, and then we'll be rewarded by getting to know our guardian spirit. One of the most effective ways to do this is with a pendulum. Select a time when you won't be disturbed. On one-inch squares of plain white paper, write each letter of the alphabet. Arrange them on a table in front of you in the proper order. Hold your pendulum and meditate for a moment. Ask the spirit to spell its name. Hold the pendulum over each letter; record any "yes" movements your pendulum makes. Hold the pendulum over each letter in this manner. When done, see if the letters you've written down make any sense to you. Thank the pendulum and try this exercise again if you wish. This takes a great deal of concentration, so don't make yourself tired. You may notice at other times, while dreaming for example, that you'll receive other messages from your guardian spirit.

James Kambos

 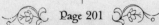

Notes:

Notes:

October 18
Thursday

 1st ♑

Color of the day: Crimson
Incense of the day: Maple

Culpeper's Birthday

Nicholas Culpeper was a six-
teenth-century physician
probably best known for his book on
herbs and herbal references. While
much of his work has been either
praised or condemned, he remains
a pioneer in the field for his work
and his insights into herbal associations and references. Now is a good
time to check our herbal cupboard
and references. It's time to start
to clean out old stock, which usually is burned at Samhain. Take an
inventory and order fresh material
to replace stale or missing herbs. It's
also time to look for new reference
material. Spruce up your herbal lore
and sharpen your personal craft.

Boudica

October 19
Friday

 1st ♑
2nd quarter 4:33 am
☽ → ♒ 12:52 pm

Color of the day: Pink
Incense of the day: Juniper

Pumpkin Spell

As Samhain approaches, it is the
proper time to decorate your
home for the holidays. Get a pumpkin to place in your front window
or on your front porch. Carve your
pumpkin in any manner you choose.
Salt some of the seeds and dry them
in your oven. Leave some unsalted
and unbaked. Put the salted seeds in
a bowl for guests to munch on, and
sprinkle the raw seeds outside for the
birds, as a gift. Place a candle inside
the pumpkin and light it at sundown,
saying:

This fire I light for
friend and kin, to let

them know they are welcome within.

May even those who can't stop a while see this face and share a smile.

Paniteowl

Notes:

happening in your area. You get the idea. Today is about doing something both inward—the soup and walk—and something outward—helping someone else. You'll feel better and more balanced for the effort than any candle gazing could possibly make you.

Laurel Reufner

Notes:

October 20
Saturday

2nd ♒
Color of the day: Blue
Incense of the day: Ginger

Make a Difference Day

This is a day to feed your soul and enjoy crisp contemplation of autumn. Make a pot of earthy soup, take a walk in the colorful out-doors, and then go do something for someone else. You can spend time at a food pantry, help an elderly or disabled neighbor, or do something useful for your parents. See if any-thing for Make a Difference Day is

October 21
Sunday

2nd ♒
☽ → ♓ 7:02 pm

Color of the day: Amber
Incense of the day: Pine

honoring the Deep

This spell honors those dark places within us where water and darkness rule. For this spell, you need to be in water physically or imagine yourself there. Try to do this ritual at night and naked, as you're going beyond the surface. Enter the water and take a moment to relax.

Let the water support and caress you. Close your eyes. What emotion comes up to the surface? Is it anger, pain, or happiness? Take note of each feeling. Do not try to solve it or keep it down, just let it flow. As the ritual ends, say a thank-you prayer:

> Thank you, spirit of water, for showing me the deep. May I use this knowledge for the betterment of myself and the world. So mote it be.

Exit the water feeling refreshed. Take what you learned and move forward. If it is something you can't handle alone, seek help.

Olivia O'Meir

Notes:

believed that their sacred isle of Avalon was the Isle of Apples; the heroes of the Nordic lands ate apples for strength and health. Modern nutrition tells us the apple is the source of many essential nutrients and promotes good health. Magically, the apple is used for love, power, and healing. Cut the apple across its waist rather than the traditional way and see the seeds arranged in a five-pointed star, the pentacle. Name each point of the pentacle for the magic you wish to invoke in a general way ("healing, magic, rest, power, love") or more specifically ("strong feet, strong hands, steady head, calm stomach, strong heart"). Chant your pentacle mindfully as you eat the apple. With each bite, chew and swallow, envisioning those things filling you.

Gail Wood

Notes:

October 22
Monday

 2nd ♓

Color of the day: Silver
Incense of the day: Coriander

Apple-A-Day Spell

Apples are sacred and special to many pantheons. The Celts

October 23
Tuesday

2nd ♓
☉ → ♏ 3:15 pm
☽ → ♈ 9:24 pm

Color of the day: Maroon
Incense of the day: Myrrh

Wreath Talisman

Select items you can find easily on the ground, or go to a craft store. Choose dried leaves, acorns, and milkweed pods, and use a hot-glue gun to attach them to a grapevine wreath. This time of year stores are filled with decorative autumn items; try to find miniature brooms to attach to the wreath. Follow this spell to make the wreath a protective symbol. Use ribbon or yarn to create a pentacle symbol in the center or fashion one from twigs.

> Wreath of autumn,
> circle round,
> Guard this space
> from harm.
> Protect all those
> within these walls,
> I dedicate this charm.

Ember

Notes:

Lore for an October day: Maples are among the most stunning trees in nature, often very bright orange and red. In October, trees are in their full glory and natural beauty (as the green of chlorophyll fades from tree leaves, only the natural color of the leaves remains). Cadmium-colored sumac gathers on roadsides and riverbanks, and provides contrast to the still-green grass and clear blue skies. The first fires have now been kindled inside to fight the coming chill at night, and days suddenly seem very short. Quilts have been pulled from cupboards to warm cold beds; our bodies begin to change in metabolism at this time of year, and our consciousness shifts from an active mental state to a psychically receptive state appropriate to the dark half of the year. This is the time of the apple harvest; and apples fill fruit bowls or are stored in the root cellar. The house is scented with applesauce laced with cinnamon. Apples have always been magically important—playing a key role in the "wassailing" ceremonies meant to ensure a bountiful harvest in the coming year. Wassail was traditionally made with hard cider heated with spices and fruit—and a ritual imbibing of this drink was likely performed at Halloween and Samhain, and at Yule. Candy apples are a modern treat celebrating the magic of the apple harvest—these treats are eaten often at Halloween even today. Bobbing for apples, too, has a long tradition as a celebratory ritual. Apples have ancient associations with healing (thus the phrase "An apple a day . . .") and were said to be useful for curing warts. The interior of an apple, sliced horizontally, reveals a five-pointed star. The final harvest of the year is the hazelnut harvest. Gather the nuts in wickerwork baskets to cure until they can be stored properly. The hazel tree was long held sacred and is symbolic of secret knowledge and divination. Forked hazel rods are useful for dowsing for sources of water or for underground minerals, and hazel is a traditional wood for magical wands.

of the men would kneel and divide it into three parts and braid them skillfully together. Reapers stood back from the sheaf and took turns throwing their reaping hooks at it. The one who was successful cried out, "Early in the morning I got on her track. Late in the evening I followed her. I have had her, I have had her!" The others then ask, "What did you have?" and he answers "*Gwrach, gwrach, gwrach*," a word meaning "hag" or "Witch." The Hag of Harvest was brought inside with much ceremony and displayed in a place of honor.

Sharynne NicMhacha

Notes:

October 24
Wednesday

2nd ♈

Color of the day: Yellow
Incense of the day: Musk

The harvest Mare

At the end of the harvest, people in Wales created a *caseg fedi* or "harvest mare," an ornament made from the last tuft of grain to be harvested. When the last sheaf of grain was standing alone in the field, one

October 25
Thursday

2nd ♈
☽ → ♉ 9:07 pm

Color of the day: Purple
Incense of the day: Neroli

Broom Consecration

Samhain is a wonderful time to get a new broom. So why not

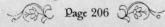

get it a few days early and do a bit of pre-festival ensorcelment? Choose or make a natural broom. Decorate it as you wish. Name your broom. Introduce yourself to it. Put your favorite music on and dance around the room with your new partner in magic—your broom! On Samhain, consecrate the broom in your tradition, and begin using it in your rituals.

Cerridwen Iris Shea

Notes:

October 26
Friday

 2nd ♉
Full Moon 12:51 am

Color of the day: Coral
Incense of the day: Carnation

Calling the Pumpkins Spell
Try carving up four small pumpkins and then tuck tea-light candles inside. Imagine using these for quarter candles on this October Full Moon. Halloween/Samhain is only a few days away—why not get

into the spirit of things and add some enchantment to your group's Full Moon celebration? Carve the pumpkins in whatever design you prefer: simple faces, stars, a triple Moon, a pentagram, or elemental symbols. As you go to place them at the quarters, try this quarter call.

> In the eastern quarter I call knowledge and intuition true.
>
> At the southern quarter I call for passion and courage in all that we do.
>
> here in the west grant us visions and bless us with love.
>
> In the north I call for security and strength from the gods above.

Ellen Dugan

Notes:

 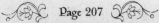

October 27
Saturday

 3rd ♉
  ☽ → ♊ 8:11 pm

Color of the day: Indigo
Incense of the day: Parsley

Confusion Clearing Coffee Spell

Mornings are usually a time of confusion. The body is waking up and the mind slowly comes alive. But what if the confusion continues? Sometimes, issues cloud our vision throughout the day due to relationship problems, job trouble, or just ordinary stress. To remedy this, pour your first cup of coffee into a yellow mug. Add sugar and say,

> To sweeten the view,
> so I may see,
> I face this vision
> objectively.

Add milk and say,

> Show me, show me.

Do not stir the coffee. Watch the milk as it settles into the coffee and see what patterns develop. While you finish your morning routine, think about how the vision applies to the problem at hand. It may be necessary to repeat the spell for best results.

Tammy Sullivan

Notes:

October 28
Sunday

 3rd ♊
  Color of the day: Gold
Incense of the day: Parsley

Sunshine Tea

Sunday is ruled by the Sun, of course, which relates to matters of health, power, and masculine energy. Associated gems include amber, topaz, ruby, and sunstone. Solar scents include marigold, heliotrope, rosemary, and frankincense. The colors of the Sun are rich yellows and oranges, especially in rayed patterns. Use this power to promote your health by making Sun tea. Stuff a cloth teabag with healthy solar herbs such as calendula, chamomile, cinnamon, ginseng, hibiscus, lemon, orange, and tea leaves. Fill a clear glass jug with cold water, add your tea bag, and say:

> As the golden hours pass,
> May Sun's power fill this
> glass.

Set in direct sunlight for several hours. Remove the tea bag, add honey to taste, and serve. This makes a wonderful ritual beverage.

Elizabeth Barrette

Notes:

October 29
Monday

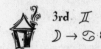

3rd ♊
☽ → ♋ 8:49 pm

Color of the day: Ivory
Incense of the day: Poplar

happy home Magical Stones

Here are a few stones to add to your home or scatter about the house to enhance your personal sacred space. Snowflake obsidian is an "un-hexing stone" that removes hex spells; place in windows or doors to prevent hex spells from entering your home. Zebra marble protects households and should be placed in the corners of the home. Goldstone (glass with flecks of copper) promotes calm; place in children's rooms to promote good, sound sleep. Sodalite also promotes peaceful sleep. Coral will protect against nightmares. Keep a piece of clear quartz and onyx next to your computer to draw away any harmful emissions and to help you to use your special tool wisely.

Boudica

Notes:

Holiday lore: Many villages in the English countryside share the tradition of "lost-in-the-dark bells." Legend tells of a person lost in the dark or fog, heading for disaster, who at the last moment was guided to safety by the sound of church bells. The lucky and grateful survivor always leaves money in his or her will for the preservation of the bells. This day commemorates one particular such case, a man named Pecket in the village of Kidderminster, in Worcestershire, who was saved from plummeting over a ravine by the bells of the local church of St. Mary's. In honor of this event, the bells still ring every October 29.

October 30
Tuesday

3rd ♋

Color of the day: Red
Incense of the day: Rose

Protective Onion Spell

Use an onion for household protection today. Sitting in the center of your home, imagine a sphere of pure white energy completely surrounding your home and family. Visualize many layers of this energy protecting and shielding you from all unwanted energies and beings. On the outside, see an orange film of added security to fortify these layers on all sides. Now go to your kitchen and cut an onion into quarters. As the tear-bringing odor reaches your nose, imagine this extra bit of defense filling the spaces between your protective energy onion. Taking the cut onion outside your home, place one quarter at each of the cardinal directions. Ask the blessings of this powerful plant, that its pieces may absorb negativity and guard against any but the most beneficial energies.

Kristin Madden

Notes:

the ubiquitous vegetable associated with this festival, then the fruit of Samhain is the magical apple. After all, can you imagine celebrating Samhain without apple bopping or candied apples? It is believed that this festival of the dead was once called the Festival of Apples, making it a perfect night for apple magic. In the story of King Arthur, upon death he was taken to Avalon, the Isle of the Apples. To help lost and wandering souls complete their journey to their own "Avalon," here is a spell: Anoint a black and orange candle with apple juice. On your altar, light the candles, saying:

> On this night, the sacred festival of the dead, may your journey complete safely once these words have been said.

Emely Flak

Notes:

October 31
Wednesday
halloween – Samhain

 3rd ♋

Color of the day: White
Incense of the day: Gardenia

Apple Magic

Tonight is Samhain, famously celebrated in mainstream culture as Halloween. If pumpkin is

November is the eleventh month of the year. Its name is derived from the Latin word for "nine," as it was the ninth month of the Roman calendar. Its astrological sign is Scorpio, the scorpion (October 23–November 23), a fixed water sign ruled by Pluto. November reveals signs of winter. The raw winds sweep up the valleys and over the hilltops. The wild grasses along the lanes are bleached to a tawny color. Nature is stripped to its bare essence. Now is a time of simple beauty. The trees reveal the shapes of their naked branches, and dried leaves flutter up the roads in the late-autumn breeze. The spirit realm is closer to us now, and more active. Dusk settles quickly. The season's first fires glow on the hearth, and blue-gray smoke curls from the chimneys. Traditional magical activities include scrying with fire, smoke, or a magic mirror. The harvest is complete, and we gather for Thanksgiving to share the bounty—especially turkey, sweet potatoes, cranberries, and pumpkin pie. November nights are magical. We can hear the stark voice of an owl hooting from out of the woods. In the darkness, the hard frost sequins the grass and the bare branches with a silver jacket—giving November's Full Moon its name, the Frost Moon. To honor her, scry into a black cauldron filled with water and one silver coin.

November 1
Thursday
Day of the Dead – All Saints' Day

 3rd ♌
$\mathcal{D} \rightarrow$ ♌ 12:48 am
4th quarter 5:18 pm

Color of the day: Green
Incense of the day: Coriander

hecate's Protection

Whenever you are in need of protection, call on Hecate, dark goddess and protector of Witches. This Greco-Roman goddess rules Heaven, Earth, and the underworld. Hecate can move through each of the three worlds easily, seeing all and knowing all. You can use this spell any time you feel threatened or unsafe.

> hecate, I call to thee.
> Watch over me
> as you can see
> all the negativity
> swarming around me.
>
> May your grace
> protect me.

The following powder will increase the power and energy of this spell. Use it to mark a sacred circle on the ground. Mix the three components in equal parts. Start with coarse sea salt for cleansing negativity. Mix in black salt (not the Indian cooking type, but the magical one) for protection.

Finally, add ground dragon's blood to complement and raise the powder's energy level.

Olivia O'Meir

Notes:

holiday lore: The time between sundown on Samhain to sundown today, the Day of the Dead, was considered a transition time, or "thin place," in Celtic lore. It was a time between the worlds when deep insights could pass more easily to those open to them. Through the portals could also pass beings of wisdom, of play, and of fun. And while in time these beings took on a feeling of otherness and evil, as our modern relationship between the realms has been muddled, today can be a day to tap into the magic and wonder of other worlds.

November 2
Friday
All Souls' Day

 4th ♌

Color of the day: Pink
Incense of the day: Sandalwood

Love for the Lost

The days immediately after Samhain are days to tend the dead. Tonight, cast a circle in your tradition of choice. Have a large pillar candle lit for the souls of the lost. Open the west gate of your circle and take time to communicate with the souls of the lost: the homeless, the orphans, the murdered, those who have no one to mourn them. Let them know they are honored and cared for, and encourage them on their journey. Close the gate once they are gone and take time in silence for yourself. Then ground, center, and open your circle.

Cerridwen Iris Shea

Notes:

November 3
Saturday

 4th ♌
☽ → ♏ 8:44 am

Color of the day: Brown
Incense of the day: Dill

November Winds Spell

Make your own wind chime out of clay. Use cookie cutters, or be original and design your own shapes. When the clay has dried, paint symbols of those things in your life that you want to change. If it's a relationship you want to change, you can simply write the person's name on one of the chimes. Use fishing line to suspend your chimes. Hang the chimes near your door, and as you hang them, say the following:

> Winds of November
> blow hard and fast,
> Into your keeping my
> cares I do cast.
> The changes you bring
> are welcome to me.
> My life will improve,
> with your help mote it
> be!

Paniteowl

Notes:

November 4
Tuesday

Daylight Saving Time ends at 2 am

 4th ♍

Color of the day: Yellow
Incense of the day: Clove

Sun Spell to Release a Painful Past

We all have memories that can still be painful to us. Use this spell to find comforting release and move forward. Harness the healing light of the Sun by using a crystal prism. Hang this crystal in a window where it catches the light and creates rainbows in the room. Sit quietly and focus on these rainbows. Think of the painful memory and imagine each rainbow as a healing laser beam, healing the wound, erasing the scar. Each time you look at one of the rainbows, smile and say:

> Shining light,
> heal my pain,
> Like the rainbow
> from the rain,
> Leave the beauty,
> take the scar,
> Like the dark
> reveals a star.

Ember

Notes:

November 5
Monday

4th ♍
☽ → ♎ 6:47 pm

Color of the day: Gray
Incense of the day: Clove

Bonfire Night Spell

In the UK this is the traditional night for bonfires, tricks and treats for children, and fireworks. Also called Guy Fawkes night, this popular autumn festival is celebrated with fires and the burning of scarecrow-looking effigies of "Guy." This is a great time to work magic for the removal of bad memories and to celebrate happier times to come. Take a slip of paper and write down the old pessimistic things you'd like to banish from your life. Add a pinch of dried lavender buds to remove negativity, and fold the paper up. Then tonight, carefully toss them in the flames of your local bonfire. Speak this charm as you do.

> Remember, remember,
> the fifth of November,
> A banishing of old hurts
> will now occur.
>
> Add a smidgen of lavender, and all will be fine,
> Making room for new memories and happier times.

Ellen Dugan

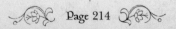

Notes:

length of white ribbon. Knot the ribbon three times. Say:

> Knot of one,
> Saint Leonard come!
>
> Knot of two,
> no theft ensue.
>
> Knot of three,
> safe are we.

Hang the blessed keys over your front door.

Lily Gardner

Notes:

November 6
Tuesday
Election Day

4th ♎

Color of the day: Black
Incense of the day: Ginger

Saint Leonard's Spell for home Security

Saint Leonard, patron saint of horses, childbirth, prisoners, and home security, is honored today. Legend has it that while the king and queen of France visited Saint Leonard, the queen went into labor. As a reward to Saint Leonard for helping the queen in childbirth, the king granted amnesty to any prisoner the saint visited. Perhaps Saint Leonard feels responsible for prisoners who, once granted freedom, return to a life of crime. In any case, he's invoked against theft. Gather three keys of any manufacture—so long as they don't unlock any door in your house. Tie them together with a

November 7
Wednesday

4th ♎

Color of the day: Topaz
Incense of the day: Ginger

Protection Amulet

During the time surrounding the great turning of the year wheel, magic would have been performed to protect against any unwanted energies, and to ensure positive influences in the newly born year. In Scotland, amulets were used for protection, either worn or carried upon the person or carefully placed in the home. Necklaces of lucky stones were created and worn, as were bracelets of leather, copper, braided hair, or red coral. Iron and rowan berries were also used, as was an amulet of senna, mint, and rue. In ancient times, the Picts (early Celtic inhabitants of northern Britain, renowned for their tattoos) created and used white quartz pebbles for healing and probably also for protection. These were quartz river stones, smoothed by the water's motion, on which were painted certain symbols or patterns in red. Create a special amulet to protect you, guide you, and bless you as you walk along the path of the Old Ones in this new year.

Sharynne NicMhacha

Notes:

November 8
Thursday

 4th ♎
☽ → ♏ 7:18 am

Color of the day: White
Incense of the day: Ginger

Inner Guru Meditation

Understanding that you have your own inner wisdom is often a journey of a lifetime. The darkest phase of the Moon provides a deep, velvety silence where past, present, and future disappear and each of us can find our own internal source of wisdom. Burn incense or essential oil that contains clary sage, and spend a little time rattling or beating a drum. Get into the sound and settle yourself into a darkened quiet space and begin breathing deeply. Quiet your mind and your drum and allow the silence to seep into your being. Cast your awareness into your heart and see a small doorway into your heart. See the doorway open and feel a welcome calling you to enter. Go through the doorway and find yourself in a special place that you know is a temple. In the middle of the room is an altar with a figure sitting in front of it in prayer. Wait patiently. When finished, the person turns and you look fully at this person. Holding out arms to you, you recognize this being as your inner guru. You go forward and stand in front of this wise person. Speaking to you, the wise one shares knowledge of your own inner wisdom and knowing. Open your heart and listen, feel, and know. When you are finished, you and the wise one bow together before the altar in prayer. Finally, the wise one bids you goodbye with a word and a bow. With one breath, you remember the word. With a second breath, you return to your space, and with a third breath, you open your eyes. Breathe in the word and remember it as a key to your own inner wisdom.

Gail Wood

Notes:

November 9
Friday

 4th ♏
New Moon 6:03 pm

Color of the day: Purple
Incense of the day: Ginger

honoring the New Moon
Tonight marks the New Moon of November. Many cultures give special names to the Moons of the year. The November Moon has gone by these and many other names: Apple Moon (Appalachian), Beaver Moon (Colonial American), Dark Moon (Celtic), Frost Moon (Almanac), Larder Moon (Stregheria), Moon When Horns Are Broken Off (Dakota), Mourning Moon (Neopagan), Remembrance Moon (Neopagan), Sassafras Moon (Choctaw), Slaughter Moon (Dutch), Snow Moon (Medieval English, Wiccan), Sorting Moon (Neopagan), Trading Moon (Cherokee), Tree Moon (Neopagan), White Moon (Chinese). Each culture marks time based on what it considers most important. Lists of twelve or thirteen lunar months tend to describe prominent seasonal events based on local weather, wildlife, or society. It gets cold and dark, apples ripen, deer shed antlers, people decide what to keep or not for the winter, festivals honor the dearly departed—all these things characterize late autumn in different places. Neopagan culture is all about reconnecting with the Earth. Today, honor the New Moon of November by giving it a name that describes what happens in your family or immediate environment. What happens to the animals, plants, and people you know at this time each year? Complete a calendar of Moons, beginning with this one.

Elizabeth Barrette

Notes:

and uncomfortable feelings into the basket. Thank her for relieving you of these things and ask that they be transformed. Then take a blessing from the basket. Hold the blessing to your heart and accept it respectfully.

Kristin Madden

Notes:

November 10
Saturday

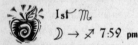

1st ♏

☽ → ♐ 7:59 pm

Color of the day: Blue
Incense of the day: Ginger

The Burden Basket

Before each sweat lodge, a friend of ours leads us all through this incredible exercise. Use it before meditation, bedtime, or anytime you wish. Imagine that the Goddess fills the sky. Her hair glistens under the light of the Sun or Moon. She pulls a single strand of hair from her head and weaves a beautiful basket from it. She calls upon the spirits and the gods to place their blessings into the basket. Then she slowly lowers it down until it hangs just before you. She tells you to place your burdens into the basket and to take a blessing from it. Place your worries, stresses,

November 11
Sunday
Veterans Day

1st ♐

Color of the day: Orange
Incense of the day: Violet

Remembrance and honor Spell

World War I was a devastating war that destroyed families and communities on all sides. The poppy fields of Flanders became soaked with the blood of thousands of dying soldiers. Red poppies became the symbol of profound grief, loss, sacrifice, and remembrance. Peace was declared on November 11 and has become a day of remem-

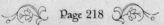

brance of all soldiers of all wars and conflicts. Gather together mementos of those who have served their country in war, disaster relief, and in peace, including photos, articles, and other sentimental items. Add to that sprigs of rosemary and lavender. Light white and silver candles. Breathe deeply and fully as you chant.

> With sacrifice of
> blood and bone
> In love and honor
> you protect us.
>
> With all honor,
> we remember
> Never judging,
> always loving.
>
> Blessed be.

Gail Wood

Notes:

istorical lore: Veterans Day commemorates the armistice that ended the Great War in 1918. Oddly, this war ended on this day, November 11, at 11 am (the 11th hour of the 11th day of the 11th month). Though Congress changed Veterans Day to another date in October at one point during this century, in 1968 they returned the holiday to November 11, where it stands today. The number 11 is significant. In numerology, it is one of the master numbers that cannot be reduced. The number 11 life path has the connotation of illumination and is associated with spiritual awareness and idealism—particularly regarding humanity. It makes sense then that this collection of 11s commemorates the end of an event that was hoped to be the War to End All Wars. Unfortunately, it wasn't the last such great war, but we can at least set aside this day to ruminate on notions of peace to humankind.

November 12
Monday

1st ♐

Color of the day: Lavender
Incense of the day: Lavender

Sea Salt Protection Spell

All Witches know that the night is a regenerative and protective force that can be harnessed. Sea salt is sacred as it comes from deep within the womb of our mother the

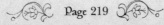

ocean goddess. While her protection is part of everyone, sometimes we need a little extra comfort. We can use charged sea salt to provide this. All you need is a bowl, salt, and a safe storage place. Pour all the salt you need to empower into the bowl. Place your hands over the bowl and chant:

> I am protected by
> your might,
> great goddess of
> day and night.

Keep chanting and building energy. When you are ready to release the energy, let the energy pour into each grain of salt. See a protective white light surrounding it. Carry the salt with you or place it on your altar. Use it whenever and wherever you need to.

Olivia O'Meir

Notes:

November 13
Tuesday

1st ♍ ↗
☽ → ♑ 8:00 am

Color of the day: Maroon
Incense of the day: Lavender

Protective Pinecones

For a beautiful and functional arrangement, try this simple technique. Gather ten pinecones. Spray paint five of them gold. Take the other five and apply spray glue to the tips. Dust with ground cloves, ginger, cinnamon, and orange zest. Tie holly leaves and pine needles in little bundles with red ribbon. Attach the pinecones to a straw wreath with wire, and tuck the greenery, along with baby's breath, into the open spaces. Place white candles nearby. As you hang the wreath, channel vibrations of protection into it. Visualize a blue light slowly surrounding the entire area. When you light the candles each night, call upon these energies and allow the blue bubble to form over the whole house.

Tammy Sullivan

Notes:

November 14
Wednesday

1st ♑

Color of the day: Yellow
Incense of the day: Evergreen

Kickstart Your Career Spell

Help kick your career into higher visibility. For this spell you will need to acquire a money Buddha and the spice essential oil of your choice. The money Buddha pose has Buddha standing with his hands over his head, holding a platter of some sort. To begin the spell, anoint Buddha on the tummy with the essential oil while telling yourself how you deserve recognition, promotion, or a pay raise. Set your Buddha in a window that receives sunlight and moonlight. Let him sit there for a full day and night. Re-anoint the little statue and keep it in your workspace.

Laurel Reufner

Notes:

November 15
Thursday

1st ♑
☽ → ♒ 6:30 pm

Color of the day: Turquoise
Incense of the day: Evergreen

Thor's Protection Spell

This day of the week is named after the Norse god Thor. Thor is a benevolent deity who is very protective and who brings abundance. Thor is visualized as a strapping and handsome man with long flowing red hair and a beard. Today is a perfect time to pull a little protection into your life and to be thankful for the things you have, all with the help of Thor. Once you acknowledge and are appreciative of Thor's influence in your life, he will continue to watch over you always.

> Thor, the Norse god of thunder, please hear this heartfelt call,
>
> I ask for your protection in the season of fall.
>
> Send abundance to me in the best possible way,
>
> May you watch over and bless me for all of my days.

Ellen Dugan

Notes:

Sprinkle the spices into the envelope, then add the yarn and seal. Hide this magical bundle in a secret place. After the spell has completed its work, build a fire. As the flames begin to grow, cast the unopened envelope into the flames. This serves to "feed" the fire, and also thanks the fire elementals for their help.

James Kambos

Notes:

November 16
Friday

 1st ≈

Color of the day: Coral
Incense of the day: Evergreen

Fireside Spell for Love

For best results, perform this spell sitting before the evening fire or a red candle. You'll need two pieces of red yarn, each about a foot long. Also have on hand a pinch each of ginger and cinnamon, and one red envelope. Hold the pieces of yarn as you think about the love you're seeking coming into your life. Slowly begin to braid the pieces of yarn together as you say:

> With this yarn I entwine;
> love hot as fire, be mine.

Lay the yarn aside. On the envelope draw a heart surrounded by flames.

November 17
Saturday

 1st ≈
2nd quarter 5:32 pm

Color of the day: Indigo
Incense of the day: Sandalwood

Shopping Success Spell

When the going gets tough, the tough go shopping—or so they say. The jokes we hear about shopping make it sound like a leisure pastime or a necessary evil. At this time of the year, with Thanksgiving around the corner and Christmas

only weeks away, we are likely to spend more time shopping for gifts. Sometimes, searching for a present for a special person can be frustrating as we look for hours without success. Saturday, ruled by the energies of Saturn, is a good day for shopping with self-control and focus. Take with you a piece of amber to help you remain focused on your mission. On a sheet of orange paper, or with an orange felt-tipped pen, write these words:

> As I venture out today,
> Please help me search
> and see
> The gifts that will
> surprise and delight
> The people who are most
> precious to me.

Carry this message with the amber in your pocket or purse.

Emely Flak

Notes:

November 18
Sunday

2nd ♒

☽ → ♓ 2:14 am

Color of the day: Gold
Incense of the day: Patchouli

Asclepius and his Guide to health

Colder weather settling in signals the watch for winter colds and flu. We may not be able to prevent these illnesses, but we can make the most magically of our sacred spaces while we recuperate. Seek aid from Asclepius and his daughter Panaceia, the goddess of remedies and herbal preparations. Take medications as prescribed by your doctor and ask Panaceia to bless them. Add generous portions of liquids and ask the blessings and aid of Asclepius. Get plenty of rest. Also invoke the aid of Asclepius's other daughter Hygiena, the goddess of good health. Her Roman adaptation is Salas, and her symbol is the pentagram. You can use her symbol for good health by scattering it about the house to keep sickness from re-entering your home.

Boudica

Notes:

November 19
Monday

2nd ♓

Color of the day: Ivory
Incense of the day: Clove

An Encouraging Spell

Everyone knows about binding spells, but most often they are used to control a negative aspect. This spell uses the same techniques, but the intent is much different. To keep something good happening in your life, you can also use a binding spell to preserve those good feelings. If you have found a job you love, and are happy with the way things are going, take something that represents your work and place it in an ice cube tray. Add water and put it in the freezer. Call on the goddess Brigit, saying,

> Mother of industry,
> hear my plea:
> May my work continue
> and be pleasing to me.
> May my labor find favor,
> and bring wealth to me.

Paniteowl

Notes:

November 20
Tuesday

2nd ♓
☽ → ♈ 6:24 am

Color of the day: Red
Incense of the day: Maple

Raven Ritual

The crow or raven is a powerful symbol of the otherworld in many traditions worldwide. They are believed to be very intelligent and have superb gifts of communication (ancient knowledge that modern science confirms). Therefore, they are often associated with prophecy or omens. Watch the activities of the corvids in your area and listen to their complex speech patterns. Create a ritual honoring the raven and enter into a deep meditative or trance-like state to see if you can begin to understand their speech. Make sure to ask the spirit of Crow or Raven beforehand, showing honor to its sacred power and asking to be shown its power or "medicine" by chanting this rune:

> Power of raven,
> spirit of crow,
> I honor your wisdom
> and all that you know.
> Wisdom of raven,
> language of crow,
> I honor the power that
> comes from below.

Sharynne NicMhacha

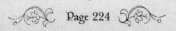

Notes:

Safe journey, safe return,
Guide me on my way.

Ember

Notes:

November 21
Wednesday

2nd ♈

Color of the day: Brown
Incense of the day: Pine

Stone Spell for Safe Travel

Many people travel during this time of year. Take a stone with you from home—it can be from your garden or driveway. Think of it as a link to your home, connecting you in order to guide you safely back again. Cleanse the stone under running water and charge it with the following chant. As you do so, visualize your safe journey and return. When you do return, replace the stone where you found it.

> From the earth you came
> to me,
> Guide me on my way.
>
> To the earth I'll bring
> you back,
> Guide me on my way.

November 22
Thursday
Thanksgiving

2nd ♈
☽ → ♉ 7:18 am
☉ → ♐ 11:50 am

Color of the day: Purple
Incense of the day: Dill

Letters of Thanksgiving

This is kind of like a Secret Santa game, in that each person in your family or group should pick one person's name from a hat about a week before Thanksgiving. Meditate on the person you chose and call to mind all that you have learned from knowing this person. Then write that person a letter expressing how thankful you are for his or her presence in your life and tell him or her just how much you care. Then, invite everyone over for a

Thanksgiving feast. Read your letters at the end of your meal and celebrate with dessert. This exercise can take a bit of courage, particularly if you are not used to freely expressing your feelings. But it opens the heart and throat chakras and deepens the bonds of love in ways you might not expect.

Kristin Madden

Notes:

November 23
Friday

2nd ♉

Color of the day: Rose
Incense of the day: Dill

Sober Stone

Around this time of the year the festive season or "silly season" brings us many opportunities to attend parties, socialize, and indulge in food and alcohol. Although we might leave home with the best intention of not consuming excess alcohol, it's easy to become carried away with the merriment of the occasion. When we are intoxicated,

particularly at a work function, we risk speaking or acting in a way that might compromise our career or professional reputation. The ancient Greeks drank from goblets made of amethyst, or placed the crystal in their drink, to minimize the effects of intoxication. If you place an amethyst in your drink at the next party you attend, you will probably attract unnecessary attention. But you can use the energies of the amethyst to help protect you from overindulgence. Carry the stone in your pocket or purse to reduce the effects of consuming excessive alcohol and to remind you of the benefits of moderation.

Emely Flak

Notes:

November 24
Saturday

2nd ♉
☽ → ♊ 6:29 am
Full Moon 9:30 am

Color of the day: Blue
Incense of the day: Ylang-ylang

Charm and Grace Spell

Short of enrolling in charm school, what can a modern Witch do to increase her personal charisma? This spell is one answer. You will need rosemary oil, a hairbrush, a red candle, a magnet, and something for etching, such as an athame. Light the red candle. Dab a tiny bit of the oil onto your palms and smooth it onto your hair. Brush your hair at least fifty strokes while chanting:

> I radiate charm
> and grace.
> My aura reflects my
> smiling face.
>
> Whomever I meet can't
> help but see
> The beauty that lies
> inside of me.

Take up the magnet and athame. Carefully etch your name into the magnet while chanting:

> I draw intelligence,
> wit, and style,
> Every second, every
> minute, every hour.
> I help others feel good
> about themselves;
> That is my special
> power.

Hold the magnet in your right hand and say:

> I call these things
> unto me.

> As I speak it,
> so mote it be!

Let the candle burn itself out while the magnet soaks up the moonlight. Dribble a bit of the wax from the candle onto the magnet and tie a few strands of hair to it as well. Carry the magnet with you at all times.

Tammy Sullivan

Notes:

November 25
Sunday

3rd ♊

Color of the day: Orange
Incense of the day: Lilac

Cleaning the House Herbs

The holidays are coming up, and this is the time of year to get your house ready for company and good times. Many pine cleaners actually contain pine oil, which is good for clearing negativity. Add some pine oil to rinse water for the bathroom and kitchen floors to draw off negativity. Use only on floors where babies will not be crawling. Add lavender to rinse water for drapes and curtains; it will leave a scent that promotes a feeling of calm and harmony. Rose oil and jasmine added sparingly to the final rinse for towels and sheets will promote a loving feeling in bath and bedroom. Continue the theme with rose soap in the bathroom. Be sure to check with your guests for allergies.

Boudica

Notes:

with cinnamon. Light the candle and focus on its flame. Imagine a bubble of red light surrounding your home, and say:

> Let the winds
> of winter shout
> As we shut
> them safely out.
>
> Let the winds
> of winter wail
> For this shield
> will never fail.
>
> Let the winds
> of winter ride
> While we all
> stay safe inside.

Blow out the candle and keep it in a safe place through the season.

Elizabeth Barrette

Notes:

November 26
Monday

 3rd ♊
$\mathbb{D} \rightarrow \mathbb{S}$ 6:07 am

Color of the day: Silver
Incense of the day: Basil

Household Holiday Protection

You've already gotten your house ready for winter. The windows are insulated, drafts blocked, appropriate fuel laid in, and so forth. But you hear that cold, cold wind gnawing at the eaves, and you still shiver. So what can you do, magically, to make the house feel warmer? You'll need a red candle, preferably scented

November 27
Tuesday

 3rd ♋

Color of the day: Gray
Incense of the day: Frankincense

The Black Mirror

If you've never worked with a black scrying mirror, this dark half of the year is a good time to start. Find a picture frame (8½ x 11 inches is a good size) that you like. Take out the glass. Wash it with a tincture of mugwort and dry it thoroughly. Paint the back of the glass a flat black and let dry thoroughly. Slide the glass back into the frame, black side to the back, and consecrate it in your tradition. Light one candle on each side of the mirror and one candle halfway between you and the center of the mirror. Gaze into the glass. Ask a specific question and let images form in the glass. Be careful not to lean forward into the flame.

Cerridwen Iris Shea

Notes:

Name-Day Spell

Everyone should take a day to celebrate his or her name. Go to: http://www.behindthename. com/namedays/ and plug your name into the "name" field. See which day or days come up. Then build a celebration around the day, using seasonal decorations, timely foods, and your favorite things. Give yourself a chance to celebrate being you.

Cerridwen Iris Shea

Notes:

November 29
Thursday

 3rd ♌

Color of the day: Crimson
Incense of the day: Juniper

A Southernwood Love Spell

This is Saint Andrew's eve. Traditionally this night was one of the most magically potent nights of the year. Throughout old Europe it was a night to perform divinations and love spells, and it was believed to be the only night of the year when vampires walked the countryside. Here is

November 28
Wednesday

 3rd ♋
☽ → ♌ 8:23 am

Color of the day: Topaz
Incense of the day: Juniper

 Page 229

a love spell appropriate for this night.
Cast your magic circle, and at each
direction light a silver candle. With
your athame, form an "X" shape
in the air above each candle. In the
center of the circle, light a red candle
you've rubbed with rose water. In
your cauldron burn the silver love-
herb, southernwood; it's an herb of
passion. Then speak this charm:

> Saint Andrew, before
> this night is through,
> hear my desire for love.
>
> This will be done with
> perfect timing, in the
> most perfect way, and
> with harm to none.

Let the red candle burn down naturally. Rub what remains of the red
candle with the cooled southernwood
ashes. Keep it as a power object if
you wish.

James Kambos

Notes:

November 30
Friday

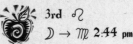

3rd ♌
☽ → ♍ 2:44 pm

Color of the day: White
Incense of the day: Carnation

holiday Peace Meditation

The holidays can be horrible.
There are so many stresses
involved: you're trying to create some
idealized experience, trying to deal
with family members who have their
own ideals, and trying to stretch
your finances. There are ways to help
banish at least some of the stress
and keep a level head to enjoy this
special time with family and friends.
Find a jar candle with a scent you
enjoy—something that speaks of
warmth, hearth, and good holiday
things. Bless the candle with bringing peace, warmth, and enjoyment to
your home. Allow it to burn each day
throughout the holiday season.

Laurel Reufner

Notes:

December is the twelfth month of the year, its name derived from the Latin for "ten," as it was the tenth month of the Roman calendar. Its astrological sign is Sagittarius, the archer (November 23–December 22), a mutable fire sign ruled by Jupiter. Winter owns the land now. Snow covers the land, and ice silences the streams. Still, this is a month of joy and renewal. Holiday lights glitter, and kitchens fill with spicy fragrances from holiday season sweets and pastries. Yule, Hanukkah, Kwanzaa, and Christmas are the holidays of December. At Yule we celebrate the return of the Sun God and burn the Yule log to honor the strengthening Sun. As we decorate the Yule tree, we honor the evergreen as a symbol of eternal life. The decorations we use on the Yule tree are rich with symbolism. The lights represent stars, fruit-shaped ornaments represent fertility, and the star atop the tree is a symbol of the divine spirit. December's Full Moon, the first of the winter season, is known as the Cold Moon. It is a white, distant Moon that shimmers above the frozen landscape. Acknowledge her by lighting a single white candle in a window. As the wheel of the year makes its final turn, we arrive at New Year's Eve, a time to honor our past and think of the future. The endless rhythm of the seasons continues.

December 1
Saturday

3rd ♏

4th quarter 7:44 am

Color of the day: Brown
Incense of the day: Nutmeg

Earth Garden Blessing

The element of earth represents the body, patience, security, and abundance. All stones stand for earth, but those especially attuned to this element include emerald, hematite, jet, moss agate, and obsidian. Earth scents include patchouli, oakmoss, cypress, magnolia, and sage. Earth colors are brown, green, and black. A good way to connect with earth is through arranging stones, sand, soil, and plants. You can make a miniature rock garden in a shallow dish with sand and several attractive stones. Or you could make a cactus garden, starting with soil, then planting cacti, finally covering with a layer of sand and one or two accent stones. Consecrate your Earth garden by concentrating on it and saying:

> Earth my own
> Garden of stone
> Maiden grown
> Mother and Crone
> I have sown
> Now I intone

> Earth my own
> Garden of stone

Notice how energy flows among the stones as in a Zen garden.

Elizabeth Barrette

Notes:

December 2
Sunday

4th ♏

Color of the day: Yellow
Incense of the day: Pine

Broken Needles Festival

The Japanese words *hari kugo* translate to "broken needles." This annual event celebrates creativity in women's crafts. We express our creativity in various ways. Some of us are creative with food, others with fabric and paper, still others through the expression of words and writing. The outcome of our creativity is the sense of achievement we feel when we complete a project. There are

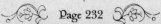

times when we need inspiration to move forward with a creative task, whether it is helping a child with a school project, finishing a photo album, designing invitations, or decorating a cake. When a deadline isn't enough to stimulate the inspiration, try this spell. Place basil or lemongrass oil on a handkerchief. Inhale the scent, recall the feeling of accomplishment you felt when you last completed a creative project, and say:

> A promise to others
> A commitment to me
>
> The outcome is
> the reward
>
> Creative completion
> it will be

Emely Flak

Notes:

December 3
Monday

 4th ♏
☽ → ♎ 1:01 am

Color of the day: Gray
Incense of the day: Parsley

Happy Holiday Card Spell

Every year during the holiday rush, we promise ourselves to start early and avoid the rush, to be more organized about writing and mailing our holiday cards. Now is the time. Gather together your address book, pens, stamps, and holiday cards and sit near some mistletoe, which is very good for achievement and attainment. Light frankincense for a favorable outcome to your holiday card project. Light a yellow candle for clarity and eloquence, and light a pink candle for harmony, friendship, and affection. Fix a cup of Earl Grey tea: the bergamot in the tea will bring you luck and accomplishment in your task. Place your hand over your cards and chant:

> In love and more,
> speed this chore.

Place your hand over your pens and say:

> Write the best words
> I've ever heard.

Then write your cards, and embellish them and the envelopes. Address and

stamp them. When all the cards are done, stack them together in a pile. Take a deep breath and send affection through your hands into the cards and say:

> Merry meet through the mail, love and greetings to you send.

Be sure to mail them the next day.

Gail Wood

Notes:

December 4
Tuesday

 4th ♎

Color of the day: Red
Incense of the day: Myrrh

Pallas Athena Day

Pallas Athena was the patron deity of Athens, and the Parthenon was her holy place. She is the goddess of both wisdom and creativity. Did you know that Athena was a patroness of craftsmen, potters, weavers, and spinners? During

the rush and bustle of preparing for the holiday season, why not think in practical terms and make a few magical gifts for friends and family? Call on Athena to help inspire you to be creative and to make a few holiday gifts this year. After all, there is nothing more thoughtful than a creative, handmade present.

> Gray-eyed Athena, patron of handmade crafts and the arts,
>
> Send your divine inspiration, let it fill up my heart.
>
> Help me to create a gift that is well thought of,
>
> Bringing happiness and joy to those that I love.

Ellen Dugan

Notes:

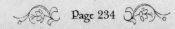

December 5
Wednesday
hanukkah begins

 4th ♎
𝄞 D → ♏ 1:31 pm

Color of the day: Topaz
Incense of the day: Dill

Shopping-Spree Spell

Place a ten-dollar bill on the desk or table where you keep your bills. Fold the bill in half and place a magnifying glass on top of the bill. See how large the bill becomes under the glass. Now think of how valuable the large bill can be. Leave the bill under the magnifying glass for three days, and each morning and evening say the following:

> Goddesses of fertility,
> come with me on my
> shopping spree.
>
> Guide my steps to
> bargains plenty; make
> my ten dollars spend
> like twenty.
>
> Let my wishes so
> prevail, that I find
> everything on sale!

Take the bill with you when you go shopping, and be sure to watch for the signs that the goddesses have heard your petition.

Paniteowl

Notes:

December 6
Thursday

 4th ♏
Color of the day: Turquoise
Incense of the day: Sandalwood

The Prosperity Candle

Candles hold a magic and mystery for us like few other things. Work with candle magic today and make your dreams come true. With a pen or pencil, inscribe your wishes into a green or gold candle. Anoint the entire candle with the essential oil of cinnamon or jasmine and sprinkle nutmeg over the oil. Ask the spirits of the nutmeg, oil, and the herbs used to create the oil for their assistance in bringing you joyful abundance. Light the candle, seeing the flame and its light releasing brilliant green and gold energies. Clearly visualize the wishes and dreams you inscribed on the candle being released to the universe, then

hold the image of these coming to fruition as long as you can. When you can no longer hold that image, release it to the flame and allow the candle to burn itself out.

                                    Kristin Madden

Notes:

December 7
Friday

4th ♏

Color of the day: White
Incense of the day: Geranium

Orange-Flower Water Spell

As a child I can remember my grandmother adding orange-flower water to holiday pastries for a delicate flavor. What I didn't know at the time is that orange-flower water can be used in spells for love, beauty, and passion, when added to a bath. Here is one such spell. Run your bath as usual. Pour a half-cup of orange-flower water (which you can buy from Middle Eastern or health food stores) into a white or clear glass bowl. Gently swirl the bowl and pray, or speak words of power for your particular need. Speak your charm three times. After blessing the orange-flower water, pour it into your bath. As you bathe, let the orange fragrance surround you. If you wish, bathe with your romantic partner. After your bath, relax and let the spell do its work.

                                    James Kambos

Notes:

Holiday lore: Cultures around the world have shared a penchant for the ritual burning of scapegoats, enemies, and devils. There is something primal about the roar of a large bonfire and its ability to bring purging light to a community. Today is such a day in the highland towns of Guatemala. Men dress in devil costumes during the season leading up to Christmas, and children chase the men through the streets. On

December 7, people light bonfires in front of their homes, and into the fires they toss garbage and other debris to purify their lives. At night, fireworks fill the air.

salt ready and drop a match into the dish. Sprinkle the basil over the fire and affirm:

> Blocks are gone,
> they are no more!
>
> Opportunity knocks
> at my door!

Sprinkle the salt over the fire to put it out.

Tammy Sullivan

Notes:

December 8
Saturday

 4th ♏
☽ → ♐ 2:11 am

Color of the day: Blue
Incense of the day: Ginger

Block Blaster Charm

It's a normal course of events to stumble upon something that blocks your path, be it a creative block, a religious dilemma, or a career with no room for advancement. Sometimes, we have to blast through those blocks so that we may continue on the path we are destined to follow. Do not wear long sleeves during this spell. Write the challenge on a slip of paper and place it in your cauldron or a fireproof dish. Pour alcohol over it. Have basil and

December 9
Sunday

 4th ♐
New Moon 12:40 pm

Color of the day: Orange
Incense of the day: Lavender

New Moon Conflict Resolution

The holidays sometimes mean family conflict. We do not always get along as we should with our family, and this ritual is all about working to overcome some of these conflicts. On white paper, write in black letters the emotions that you feel may surface as you come in contact with some of your family members. Maybe even go so far as to write down specific issues that exist between yourself and these family members. Gather together a fireproof tray or cauldron, a black candle for protection, and yellow and white candles for peace and resolution. Create your sacred space, and call upon Hestia to join you. Light the candles. Talk to her about what you would like to achieve. Then take your papers and burn them on the fireproof tray or in your cauldron. Release these issues and emotions as you watch the flames eat the papers. Give thanks to Hestia, and ask that she remain to help you over the sticky issues that may arise. Finish by clearing your sacred space.

                                Boudica

Notes:

December 10
Monday

 1st ♐

☽ → ♑ 1:50 pm

Color of the day: Lavender
Incense of the day: Lavender

holiday Preparation Spell

Gather together a notepad, paper, an address book, gift lists, cookbooks, boxes of holiday cards, a piece of holiday wrapping paper (9 x 9 inches), and a ribbon. Take one blue, one orange, and one white candle in candleholders. Rub your favorite essential oil on them and have a tiny vial of that oil with your spell components. Light the blue candle, saying:

A light for serenity.

Light the orange candle, stating:

A light for stamina.

Now light the white candle, stating:

A light for joy.

Hold your hands over your pile of objects. Close your eyes, visualizing a joyful, organized, and productive time. Feel the energy radiate from your hands into the objects. Open the vial of oil and inhale deeply. This scent connects you to the positive experience. Carry the vial with you always until Twelfth Night. Any time you feel stressed or blue, open it and inhale, remembering the feeling. Burn the candles all the way down.

Write a wish on the inside of the holiday paper. Fold it into thirds. Tie it with the ribbon and hang it where you can see it all season.

                    Cerridwen Iris Shea

Notes:

Then go check the batteries in your smoke detector and make sure it's working.

                    Laurel Reufner

Notes:

December 11
Tuesday

 1st ♑

Color of the day: White
Incense of the day: Rose

Mistletoe Protection Charm

Along with festivities, the holiday season also brings extra hazards as we fill our homes with Yule trees, lights, and even more candles than usual. Mistletoe is a historical protection from fire. Charge a sprig of mistletoe for added protection to your home, and then hang it from a central point in the house. You could also hang it in the room with the most added fire hazards.

December 12
Wednesday
hanukkah ends

1st ♑

Color of the day: Yellow
Incense of the day: Dill

Genuine Success Spell

Use this spell to ensure a productive career or business venture. You do not have to have a materialistic or strictly monetary goal in mind. We all need and deserve to make a living in this world to provide for our families and keep a home to live in. Keep this charm at your place of work or in a place where you'll see it every day, such as on an altar or in the vehicle you drive to work. Cleanse a piece of citrine quartz and charge it with the following purpose:

May this business that
I'm in be blessed,
With pleasure, good will,
and success.

May good fortune look
upon my work,
And guide my efforts
without hurt.

Let abundance
come to me,
For the good of all,
so mote it be.

                              Ember

Notes:

be used in unusual ways. The clear
glass Christmas tree ornaments are
excellent for making Witch balls.
Take the hanger cap off and fill the
ornament with needles, pins, colored
tacks, fingernail clippings, a lock of
your hair, and bright beads. Replace
the cap, using super glue to ensure
that all of bits and pieces are locked
inside. Now bury the ball near your
front door, saying:

> None will see this
> bit of glass,
> where only friends will
> tend to pass.
>
> Yet should one
> come in enmity,
> let them stumble,
> so mote it be!

                              Paniteowl

Notes:

December 13
Thursday

 1st ♑

☽ → ♒ 12:01 am

Color of the day: Purple
Incense of the day: Eucalyptus

Witch's Ball of Protection
Wonderful things can be found
in this holiday season that can

December 14
Friday

 1st ≈

Color of the day: Pink
Incense of the day: Musk

Overcoming Relationship Blocks

Use this spell to break through and destroy communication blocks that hurt your relationships. Communication blocks can hurt every relationship—even the ones you have with yourself—so it's important to try to keep the lines of communication open. Here are a few quick ideas. At the beginning of the talk, light a yellow, white, or blue candle. The yellow or white candles will bring clarity of thought and words. Blue candles promote peace and harmony. In addition, say a little prayer out loud or to yourself. Ask the God and Goddess for clarity of thought, honesty, and understanding. In times when you can't light a candle, just say the prayer to yourself and see a flame being lit on the astral plane, glowing in the appropriate colors.

Olivia O'Meir

Notes:

December 15
Saturday

 1st ≈

☽ → ♓ 8:15 am

Color of the day: Indigo
Incense of the day: Almond

All-That-Is Meditation

In the United States, the first ten amendments of the Constitution, the Bill of Rights, are celebrated on this day as the Bill of Rights Day. Similarly, the United Nations has made this day Human Rights Day. Each of these celebrations reminds us that our rights and freedoms as citizens of our countries have often come after very hard work and sacrifice by others. As children of Mother Earth, we also realize that all creatures of the Earth are entitled to acknowledgement as sacred beings. As we seek our rights as humans, we are mindful that these rights extend to the other creatures within the web of life. Light jasmine incense for connections and take a deep breath, moving into a deep meditative state. Find yourself standing out in the dark, limitless void. You are safe and unafraid as you stand in this infinite darkness. In front of you, you see a shining thread of life and see it connect to someone you love; then you see another shining thread of life connecting you to someone you don't know. The threads increase one by one, connecting you to other people, to animals, to plants, and to rocks and other natural beings. Patiently you allow these threads to unwind, move out, and connect. Onward and outward they go. Finally these threads stop, and you are able to see your connections to all. Take very deep breaths and breathe in those connections. Feel the heartbeats and vibrations of the others; feel the deep harmony and love of the universe that surrounds you. When you are finished, thank all the beings present and disconnect yourself from these threads. Open your eyes, ground and center, and go about your day.

Gail Wood

Notes:

December 16
Sunday

 1st ♓

Color of the day: Yellow
Incense of the day: Coriander

Mincemeat Pie Season

The origins of mincemeat pie go back to the Egyptians, who baked this pastry in the shape of a little coffin to honor Osiris on the winter solstice. The Crusaders brought mincemeat back with them to Europe in the eleventh century, and it became the traditional Yuletide treat. In the seventeenth century, the Puritans tried their best to outlaw the pies, calling them "idolatry in crust." It is said that for every slice of mincemeat pie that you eat, you will have a lucky month in the coming year. The only condition is that each pie you partake of must be baked by a different cook. The magical properties of mincemeat are: apples for love and health, raisins and nuts for prosperity, fruit peel and sugar for love, ginger for money, cinnamon and nutmeg for psychic awareness, and rum for protection.

Lily Gardner

Notes:

December 17
Monday

 1st ♓
2nd quarter 5:17 am
☽ → ♈ 1:52 pm

Color of the day: Ivory
Incense of the day: Cinnamon

Relaxing Ritual

With so much celebration going on this month, our bodies need as much cleansing as our spirits do. While not everyone has access to a sauna or sweat lodge, a body scrub and warm (or hot) bath can be a good second choice for relaxation and release of toxins from body and mind. Mix together 4 tablespoons sea salt, 2 tablespoons olive oil, 1 tablespoon lemon juice, and, if you like, an eighth of a teaspoon of eucalyptus or jasmine essential oil. Make this into a watery paste and scrub it over your body. Leave it on for 10 minutes and rinse off. Or better yet, add 1 cup of strong chamomile tea and 1 cup powdered milk to a warm bath and wash off your body scrub in that before taking a long, relaxing soak.

Kristin Madden

Notes:

Holiday lore: Saturnalia was the Roman midwinter celebration of the solstice, and the greatest of the Roman festivals. It was traditional to decorate halls with laurels, green trees, lamps, and candles. These symbols of life and light were intended to dispel the darkness of the season of cold. The festival began with the cry of "Io Saturnalia!" Young pigs were sacrificed at the temple of Saturn and then were served the next day. Masters gave slaves the day off and waited on them for dinner. Merrymaking followed as wine flowed and horseplay commenced. Dice were used to select one diner as the honorary "Saturnalian King." Merrymakers obeyed absurd commands to dance, sing, and perform ridiculous feats. It was also a tradition to carry gifts of clay dolls and symbolic candles on one's person to give to friends met on the streets.

 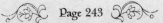

December 18
Tuesday

2nd ♈

Color of the day: Black
Incense of the day: Peony

Yuki–Onna Snow Spell

Snow is the bane and blessing of winter. If you have to shovel it off your sidewalk, it's a bane. But if you plan to go skiing, or build snowmen, or host a snowball fight—then snow is essential. Yuki-Onna, or Oyuki, is the Japanese spirit of snow. She rules winter; her tears turn into snowflakes. If she finds travelers lost in a blizzard, she can guide them to safety, but she can also freeze anyone who offends her. To win her favor, try offerings such as sweet rice cakes or rice wine, or read tragic poetry. Also decorate your altar with snowflakes of cut or folded paper. Then say:

> Yuki–Onna, come
> dancing tragedy and hope
> weeping snow and wind

It is prudent to explain how much snow you want, so you don't summon a two-foot blizzard when six inches would suffice!

Elizabeth Barrette

Notes:

December 19
Wednesday

2nd ♈

☽ → ♉ 4:38 pm

Color of the day: Brown
Incense of the day: Sage

Open Your Options Spell

This spell energizes your career options by widening our perspective so that we may see other possibilities. Draw a warm bath. Add blessed salt, jasmine, roses, and vanilla to the water. Settle into the bath and let the warm water soak into your skin. Delight in the aroma. Breathe the healing steam. After about ten minutes begin to chant:

> All is not as it may seem.
> I wish to see everything!

After chanting for several minutes, in a normal voice state your purpose:

> I wish to see all of my
> career options.

Allow your face and whole body to slip into the water with your eyes open. Count to ten and come to the surface to breathe. Do this nine times in a row.

Tammy Sullivan

Notes:

December 20
Thursday

 2nd ♉

Color of the day: Crimson
Incense of the day: Cedar

Goddess of the Last-Minute Shoppers

If you are still shopping, chances are you do this every year—and it's hard to find anything so close to the holidays. Call upon Sadie, Goddess and Queen of the Bargain Shoppers, to help you search for the perfect gift at the ideal price. She can be found in any department store. She is that lady you see only from the back, both hands filled with shopping bags from every store in town. Only a secret goddess like Sadie could stand up to the last-minute shopping crush and find the bargains and the-last-one-of-its-kind, just-the-right-size-and-color, got-to-have-this-toy items. Follow her as she leads you to the best bargain racks, helping you find exactly the right gift for that special person.

Boudica

Notes:

December 21
Friday

 2nd ♉
☽ → ♊ 5:14 pm

Color of the day: Purple
Incense of the day: Vanilla

Venus Meditation

This time of year is often very busy, filled with the joy of doing things for others. But sometimes people overextend themselves and end up tired and stressed. The goddess Venus has sometimes been described as selfish and demanding, but there are times when we need to be a little selfish and do something nice for ourselves so we can be available to others. Pamper yourself with a bath by wrapping the following in cheesecloth: one chamomile tea bag, dried thyme, lavender, and peppermint. Add the bag to the bath water. Light candles in various shades of green and pink and use bubble bath if you desire. Play relaxing music or do whatever it takes to relax, even if it's just for a few minutes. Visualize both the strong and the loving characteristics of Venus, which will increase your ability to share love with others.

Ember

Notes:

December 22
Saturday
Yule – Winter Solstice

 2nd ♊

☉ → ♑ 1:08 am

Color of the day: Blue
Incense of the day: Vanilla

Light of the World Spell

For this spell, you will need a small globe of the world (even one as small as a pencil sharpener will work) and three white candles in candle holders. Set the candles in a triangle around the globe. Light the candles in clockwise order, starting at the top. Take a snuffer and extinguish the candles, counterclockwise, saying:

> The longest night,
> winter of the soul.

In the dark, contemplate the positive changes you wish to see in the world. When ready, light the candles clockwise, saying:

> From the depths of the
> soul comes hope,
> light of the world.

Spin the globe, visualizing the positive changes. Let the candles burn all the way down. Keep the globe to use in spellwork that enhances the Earth.

Cerridwen Iris Shea

Notes:

Holiday lore: The Yule season is a festival of lights, and a solar festival, and is celebrated by fire in the form of the Yule log—a log decorated with fir needles, yew needles, birch branches, holly sprigs, and trailing vines of ivy. Back porches are stacked with firewood for burning, and the air is scented with pine and wood smoke. When the Yule log has burned out, save a piece for use as a powerful amulet of protection through the new year. Now is a good time to light your oven for baking bread and confections to serve around a decorated table; sweets have an ancient history. They are made and eaten to ensure that one would have "sweetness" in the coming year. Along these lines, mistletoe hangs over doorways to ensure a year of love. Kissing under the mistletoe is a tradition that comes down from the Druids, who considered the plant sacred. They gathered mistletoe from the high branches of sacred oak with golden sickles. It is no coincidence that Christians chose this month to celebrate the birth of their savior Jesus. Now is the time when the waxing Sun overcomes the waning Sun, and days finally begin to grow longer again. In some Pagan traditions, this struggle is symbolized by the Oak King overcoming the Holly King—that is, rebirth once again triumphing over death. And so the holly tree has come to be seen as a symbol of the season. It is used in many Yuletide decorations. For instance, wreaths are made of holly, the circle of which symbolized the wheel of the year—and the completed cycle. (*Yule* means "wheel" in old Anglo-Saxon.)

Yule Moon Spell

Prepare a Yule log. If you don't have a place to burn an open fire, an oak log can be used with a candle to symbolize the Yule fire. Drill a hole in the log big enough to hold a candleholder. Place a bayberry candle in the holder, and place holly leaves on the log. If you can have an open fire, use bayberry and holly leaves in your fire pit. Light your fire, saying:

> By oak and holly,
> let no one's folly
> blight this home
> of love and cheer.

Light your fire, or candle, at sundown, and sit by it as it burns away. Think of all the things you've learned over the past year, and plan ahead for all the new things coming your way in the coming year.

Paniteowl

Notes:

December 23
Sunday

2nd ♊

☽ → ♋ 5:18 pm

Full Moon 8:15 pm

Color of the day: Amber
Incense of the day: Violet

December 24
Monday
Christmas Eve

 3rd ♋

Color of the day: Silver
Incense of the day: Sage

The Charge of the Goddess

Thanks to Charles Godfrey Leland and Doreen Valiente, Witches have a lovely piece of sacred writing called "The Charge of the Goddess." The Charge was first recorded in Leland's *Aradia: Gospel of the Witches*. Valiente was moved by the piece, so she rewrote it with a more Wiccan feel. The Charge is the Goddess speaking directly to a ritual's participants after she has been invoked. While the well-known copies of the Charge are moving, each Witch can and should write her own version to reflect her personal beliefs. Here are some tips to help you write your charge: meditate about on the way the Goddess manifests in nature; your connection to nature; the cycle of life, death, and rebirth; or focus on a specific aspect of her. However, the most important thing to remember when writing a charge is to write from your soul, where the Goddess lives.

Olivia O'Meir

Notes:

December 25
Tuesday
Christmas

 3rd ♋
☽ → ♌ 6:52 pm

Color of the day: White
Incense of the day: Chrysanthemum

Thankful Meditation

This is a season during which we are told to be thankful. Today in particular is a good day to consider all the things in our lives that bring us joy, peace, and yes, thankfulness. Get yourself a journal and a pen you like. If you wish, write a dedication or blessing on the first page. Then date another page and begin listing the things you are glad to have in your life. Continue the process by taking some time on the good days to make other lists. When you have a bad day, brew up a cup of tea or pot of coffee, get out your journal, and spend some time revisiting the good things in your life.

Laurel Reufner

Notes:

ate and sprinkle some of the seeds onto the paper. Fold the paper as you would a letter. Place it into an envelope and seal with some of the juice from the pomegranate. Speak a prayer of thanks over the burning candle before extinguishing it. Save the letter until the wishes manifest. The custom is to save your wish list until the following year; review to see what happened to your wishes before burning it in a ritual fire.

James Kambos

Notes:

December 26
Wednesday
Kwanzaa begins

3rd ♌

Color of the day: Topaz
Incense of the day: Gardenia

End of the Year Wishes Spell

Since this is the last Wednesday of the year, it is a good day to communicate to the divine what you wish for during the coming year. Perform this spell at sunrise on the Wednesday closest to the New Year. Light a yellow candle and call upon Mercury, messenger of the gods. Write your wishes in the form of affirmations on clean white paper. This may be in the form of a spell, prayer, or letter. After you write the spell, cut a pomegran-

December 27
Thursday

 3rd ♌
☽ → ♍ 11:44 pm
2nd Quarter 9:48 am

Color of the day: Green
Incense of the day: Neroli

Releasing Old Bonds Ritual

This spell will break old harmful bonds with another person so you can begin anew. You'll need scissors, one black and one white candle, a picture of yourself and the other person, and a silver ribbon. Set up the altar with the scissors across the top, white candle on the right and black on the left, and the pictures and ribbon in the center. Light the black candle to represent the negative aspects of the relationship and the white candle for the positive ones. Tie the pictures together with the ribbon, with one end around your picture and the other around the picture of the other party. Now, quickly cut the ribbon with the scissors. Let go of anger and hate. Let love and peace fill your memories. Declare the bond to be broken with blessings as your lives go separate ways. Bury the candles and place the pictures in a moving body of water to represent moving on.

Olivia O'Meir

Notes:

December 28
Friday

 3rd ♏

Color of the day: Rose
Incense of the day: Geranium

Receiving Love Spell

Friday is named for the Norse goddess Freya, who, like Venus, is a goddess of love. It is said that her tears produced gold when they fell on rock, amber when shed at sea. Find a piece of amber or an item of amber jewelry—a heart-shaped piece would be ideal, but is not necessary. Amber is reputed to make its wearer irresistible. Use this spell to bring out your inner beauty and make yourself open to receiving love. This spell can be helpful in strengthening all types of loving relationships—romantic, family, and friends. Cleanse the amber beneath running water and dry it gently with a soft towel. Charge the amber to bring out its loving qualities:

> Amber tears that
> Freya shed
> Floating in the sea.
>
> Amber that I
> hold in hand,
> Bring loving
> qualities to me.

For giving and
receiving love
Grant me this,
so mote it be.

Ember

Notes:

celebrate what we did complete. In your journal or in a notebook, write down everything you accomplished. Every small achievement or completion counts. Congratulate yourself and reflect on how each experience has enriched your knowledge and personal development. Give thanks to the deities for your ongoing learning journey. Do the same activity with a close friend and congratulate each other. Now celebrate with your favorite beverage. Well done!

Emely Flak

Notes:

December 29
Saturday

 3rd ♍

Color of the day: Gray
Incense of the day: Nutmeg

An Accomplished Meditation

Today the Moon is in its waning phase just as the calendar year comes to a close. Before setting goals for the new year ahead, this is an ideal time to reflect on what has taken place over the last year. Although it's important to reflect on what you would do differently if you had the time again, it's even more necessary that you think about what you have achieved. We are often critical of our achievements or lament what we didn't achieve rather than

December 30
Sunday

3rd ♍
☽ → ♎ 8:37 am

Color of the day: Gold
Incense of the day: Lavender

Irish Blessing

Here is a traditional Irish blessing you can use every day, or at the end of your circles:

May the blessing of light be with you; light within and light without.

May sunlight shine upon you and warm your heart 'til it glows like a great peat fire, so that the stranger may come and be warmed by it.

May a blessed light shine out of your two eyes, like a candle set in the window, bidding the wanderer to come in out of the storm.

May you ever give a kindly greeting to those you meet along the path.

May the blessing of rain fall upon you, so that flowers spring up to shed their sweetness in the air, and may the bless-ings of the Earth, the good, rich Earth, be with you always.

Sharynne NicMhacha

Notes:

December 31
Monday
New Year's Eve

 3rd ♎
4th quarter 2:51 am

Color of the day: White
Incense of the day: Nutmeg

A New Year's Affirmation

A few minutes before midnight, light a white candle to symbol-ize the new year. Then set it in a prominent place and move to your front door. Open the door wide and say the spell as the new year is born.

> As the clock strikes twelve, so begins a new calendar year.
>
> Now ring in prosperity, health, happiness, and good cheer.
>
> I welcome this magical year with hope and open arms.
>
> May I keep my vows to help, to heal, and to cause no harm.
>
> By the powers of hearth and home this spell is spun,
>
> As I will it so shall it be, and let it harm none.

Ellen Dugan

A Guide to Witches' Spell-A-Day Icons

 New Moon Spells

 New Year's Eve, Day

 Imbolc

 Valentine's Day

 Ostara, Easter

 April Fool's Day

 Earth Day

 Beltane

 Mother's Day

 Father's Day

 Litha

 Lammas

 Mabon

 Full Moon Spells

 Samhain, Halloween

 Thanksgiving

 Yule, Christmas

  Health Spells

 Home and Garden Spells

 Protection Spells

 Travel and Communication Spells

 Money and Success Spells

 Love and Relationship Spells

Grab Bag of Spells

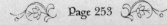

Daily Magical Influences

Each day is ruled by a planet that possesses specific magical influences:

Monday (Moon): peace, healing, caring, psychic awareness, and purification.

Tuesday (Mars): passion, sex, courage, aggression, and protection.

Wednesday (Mercury): conscious mind, study, travel, divination, and wisdom.

Thursday (Jupiter): expansion, money, prosperity, and generosity.

Friday (Venus): love, friendship, reconciliation, and beauty.

Saturday (Saturn): longevity, exorcism, endings, homes, and houses.

Sunday (Sun): healing, spirituality, success, strength, and protection.

Lunar Phases

The lunar phase is important in determining best times for magic. Times are Eastern Standard Time.

The waxing Moon (from the New Moon to the Full Moon) is the ideal time for magic to draw things toward you.

The Full Moon is the time of greatest power.

The waning Moon (from the Full Moon to the New Moon) is a time for study, meditation, and little magical work (except magic designed to banish harmful energies).

Astrological Symbols

The Sun	☉	Aries	♈
The Moon	☽	Taurus	♉
Mercury	☿	Gemini	♊
Venus	♀	Cancer	♋
Mars	♂	Leo	♌
Jupiter	♃	Virgo	♍
Saturn	♄	Libra	♎
Uranus	♅	Scorpio	♏
Neptune	♆	Sagittarius	♐
Pluto	♇	Capricorn	♑
		Aquarius	♒
		Pisces	♓

The Moon's Sign

The Moon's sign is a traditional consideration for astrologers. The Moon continuously moves through each sign in the zodiac, from Aries to Pisces. The Moon influences the sign it inhabits, creating different energies that affect our daily lives.

Aries: Good for starting things, but lacks staying power. Things occur rapidly, but quickly pass. People tend to be argumentative and assertive.

Taurus: Things begun now do last, tend to increase in value, and become hard to alter. Brings out an appreciation for beauty and sensory experience.

Gemini: Things begun now are easily changed by outside influence. Time for shortcuts, communications, games, and fun.

Cancer: Stimulates emotional rapport between people. Pinpoints need, supports growth and nurturance. Tend to domestic concerns.

Leo: Draws emphasis to the self, to central ideas or institutions, away from connections with others and emotional needs. People tend to be melodramatic.

Virgo: Favors accomplishment of details and commands from higher up. Focus on health, hygiene, and daily schedules.

Libra: Favors cooperation, compromise, social activities, beautification of surroundings, balance, and partnership.

Scorpio: Increases awareness of psychic power. Precipitates psychic crises and ends connections thoroughly. People tend to brood and become secretive under this Moon sign.

Sagittarius: Encourages flights of imagination and confidence. This Moon sign is adventurous, philosophical, and athletic. Favors expansion and growth.

Capricorn: Develops strong structure. Focus on traditions, responsibilities, and obligations. A good time to set boundaries and rules.

Aquarius: Rebellious energy. Time to break habits and make abrupt change. Personal freedom and individuality is the focus.

Pisces: The focus is on dreaming, nostalgia, intuition, and psychic impressions. A good time for spiritual or philanthropic activities.

Glossary of Magical Terms

Altar: a low table that holds magical tools as a focus for spell workings.

Athame: a ritual knife used to direct personal power during workings or to symbolically draw diagrams in a spell. It is rarely, if ever, used for actual physical cutting.

Aura: an invisible energy field surrounding a person. The aura can change color depending upon the state of the individual.

Balefire: a fire lit for magical purposes, usually outdoors.

Casting a circle: the process of drawing a circle around oneself to seal out unfriendly influences and raise magical power. It is the first step in a spell.

Censer: an incense burner. Traditionally, a censer is a metal container, filled with incense, that is swung on the end of a chain.

Censing: the process of burning incense to spiritually cleanse an object.

Centering yourself: to prepare for a magical rite by calming and centering all of your personal energy.

Chakra: one of the seven centers of spiritual energy in the human body, according to the philosophy of yoga.

Charging: to infuse an object with magical power.

Circle of protection: a circle cast to protect oneself from unfriendly influences.

Crystals: quartz or other stones that store cleansing or protective energies.

Deosil: clockwise movement, symbolic of life and positive energies.

Deva: a divine being according to Hindu beliefs; a devil or evil spirit according to Zoroastrianism.

Direct/Retrograde: refers to the motions of the planets when seen from the Earth. A planet is "direct" when it appears to be moving forward from the point of view of a person on the Earth. It is "retrograde" when it appears to be moving backward.

Dowsing: to use a divining rod to search for a thing, usually water or minerals.

Dowsing pendulum: a long cord with a coin or gem at one end. The pattern of its swing is used to predict the future.

Dryad: a tree spirit or forest guardian.

Fey: an archaic term for a magical spirit or a fairylike being.

Gris-gris: a small bag containing charms, herbs, stones, and other items to draw energy, luck, love, or prosperity to the wearer.

Mantra: a sacred chant used in Hindu tradition to embody the divinity invoked; it is said to possess deep magical power.

Needfire: a ceremonial fire kindled at dawn on major Wiccan holidays. It was traditionally used to light all other household fires.

Pentagram: a symbolically protective five-pointed star with one point upward.

Power hand: the dominant hand, the hand used most often.

Scry: to predict the future by gazing at or into an object such as a crystal ball or pool of water.

Second sight: the psychic power or ability to forsee the future.

Sigil: a personal seal or symbol.

Smudge/Smudge stick: to spiritually cleanse an object by waving incense over and around it. A smudge stick is a bundle of several incense sticks.

Wand: a stick or rod used for casting circles and as a focus for magical power.

Widdershins: counterclockwise movement, symbolic of negative magical purposes, sometimes used to disperse negative energies.

Spell Notes: